These are stories of faith being shaped. We are indebted to these writers for stories that flesh out an incarnate God present when a pastor and congregant meet. Powerful stories make powerful faith.

Gil Rendle, The Alban Institute

With candor, wisdom, and engaging narrative styles, the contributors to this volume tell the truth about life in the pews. Pastors often say they want to know how people in congregations really experience the faith. I cannot imagine a more compelling place to encounter that reality than in this book.

Thomas G. Long, Candler School of Theology

These lively memoirs reflect, inform, warn, and bless. They confirm the old, old story: God's best ministry is always in flesh and blood.

Cornelius Plantinga, Calvin Theological Seminary

Speaking of Pastors

Parishioners Tell Their Stories

edited by James Schaap

Christian Reformed Church in North America
Grand Rapids, Michigan

We welcome your comments. Call us at 1-877-279-9994 X0805 or e-mail us at pastoralexcellence@crcna.org .

Cover design by Frank Gutbrod

ISBN 978-0-9753387-1-1

Contents

Editor's Preface

Twenty-five years ago I was a young man and the Christian Reformed Church in North America was, in my estimation, quite a different denomination. We've both changed, and that we have should surprise no one. Change is in the nature of things; nothing stays the same, save the love of God.

I'm not sure how this all came about, but somehow—there was some connection with the 125th denominational birthday—I was given the enviable job of surveying the state of the denominational union by writing stories about 35 somewhat randomly chosen individuals from all over the continent. Who are we? What are we up to? What do we think of ourselves?—those kinds of questions I asked each subject, while also describing at least some aspect of their lives. The result was a *Banner* series and a book titled *CRC Family Portrait*, an album of stories about the lives of folks who were, back then, God's people called Christian Reformed, as Andrew Kuyvenhoven used to call us.

The divisive issues of the subsequent decades were beginning to emerge at the time, although a decade or more would pass before seams would split and some fellowships would be torn asunder. Nevertheless, when I asked my subjects one of the questions I always did—"what do you consider the strengths and weaknesses of the denomination?" their answers often referenced some of the trials then looming and were offered, frequently, in theological language.

Both north and south of the border, I was somewhat surprised, however, at how often I heard the same answer given to the question of relative strengths. Time after time people answered, "the preaching of the Word." Again and again, people I met made clear what they considered the heart of things; over and over again, they insisted it was preaching—which means, of course, preachers.

One man, a farmer, answered the question so forcefully that the table at which we were sitting shook when he pounded his fist. "In our church, the preacher still stands up on the pulpit and says, 'Thus saith the Lord.'"

Were I to begin a similar project today, my guess is that I wouldn't hear that answer so frequently. I'm not sure what answer I might receive; in fact,

I'm not sure I'd get any consistent answer at all. Chances are people would refer specifically to their own particular congregation's particular strengths.

Twenty-five years ago, only our sociologists could have predicated the demise of denominationalism in North America. Back then, the CRCs' ethnic bonds definitively linked churches in the family, from Zeeland to Abbotsford. Today, whatever glue our Dutch origins brought to the denominational life is slowly but surely loosening. Bonds are demonstrably weaker, frequently non-existent. We travel more easily and communicate around the world by clicking a mouse. More people bowl alone these days. More people form communities—real or virtual—in ways that would have been unimaginable in 1980.

So I shouldn't be surprised, I suppose, that the essays you're about to read don't speak often about "the preaching of the Word."

The assignment I posed to each of the writers was easy enough: write a good strong essay, full of specific examples, about life in the pew, about living there Sunday after Sunday, about being preached to and being pastored. Once you read what's between the covers of this book, you may be surprised, as I was, to see how few contributors said much at all about preaching. One particularly beautiful contribution places "the preaching of the Word" at the very heart of things; but if you read that essay carefully, you will note that the conclusion comes somewhat grudgingly.

Most of the stories, most of the advice, most of the direction you'll find between the covers of this book concern the importance of interpersonal relationships. But then we live in a therapeutic age, in a time when the particular jargon of a hundred different therapies has found its way into ordinary conversation. In education, collaboration is in; lectures are not. In worship, multiple voices and various forms of media often characterize those fellowships which push out the cutting edge of evangelical life; a single voice, up front, holding forth, represents the kind of authority that seems, well, early 20th century. I am sometimes amazed that preaching can survive at all in an increasingly MTV world.

But then there's this. Not long ago on a Sunday morning, my wife—as is her great joy—took the hand of our four-year-old granddaughter to begin the three-block walk home to Grandma's house. It was January, and at the coat rack, the two of them came face to face with the preacher.

"Well, Jocelyn," he said, bending down to look into my granddaughter's eyes. "How are you this morning?"

She said nothing, which didn't surprise her grandmother. But she smiled, which is all the preacher was likely even looking for.

When he walked away, Jocelyn looked up at her Grandma quizzically. "How does he know my name?" she said, almost as if she were shocked.

That story is the nutshell of this entire collection of essays, and may well serve as a gateway to your reading. What seems clear from the voices you'll hear is that, at least from the vantage of the pew today, pastors—preachers—need to earn the right to be heard. The demise of authority in a post-modern age brings institutions low—including the church. A preacher simply doesn't have authority on the basis of occupation or education, as he once did, as my grandfather did when he walked into the pulpit with his swallow-tail coat. A preacher has to earn the authority necessary to hold forth—and he or she does that on the basis of the respect and love he gives to others on a personal basis.

That's something easier said than done perhaps, but the burden of this book of essays is to deliver stories that will help all of us understand how that authority may be gained—what must be avoided, what must be nurtured.

Don't be deceived, however. *Speaking of Pastors* is still very much a book about preaching, although it may be just a bit more about ministering.

Our hope and prayer is that the stories recounted in the essays in this book help us all, pastors and lay folks, bring praise to our God, who wants, really, nothing more.

This collection of narratives is part of a larger project known as Sustaining Pastoral Excellence (SPE), a program funded by Lilly Endowment Inc., that seeks to support pastors by helping them build vital congregations.

The SPE implementation team of the Christian Reformed Church seeks to promote healthy pastors and congregations by providing resources for mentoring, peer learning, and continuing education. In connection with these efforts, the implementation initially produced a volume of essays by pastors, stories which narrate the experiences that spoke to the issue of persevering in ministry. That volume, *Persevering in Ministry: Pastors Tell Their Stories* (Grand Rapids, MI: Christian Reformed Church in North America, 2004) was edited by Joel Kok.

The book you have in your hands, *Speaking of Pastors: Parishioners Tell Their Stories,* was the brainchild of the SPE implementation team, who thought a companion volume from the other side of the pulpit might be in order, both to instruct and delight.

Both volumes are meant to help us all go about the task of sustaining pastoral excellence.

A Note to Readers

At the end of each chapter in this book you will find a section called "For Further Reflection." The purpose of these sections is to encourage you to read and discuss this book in some kind of communal setting. Possibilities for such settings include: pastors and their councils, beginning pastors and their mentors, small groups or book clubs within congregations, seminarians, groups of pastors who have gathered for mutual edification, and any group of believers who love the church and its leaders. The narratives and the reflections embedded in them can stimulate church members to reflect on what God is teaching them as their own stories unfold. Reading this book in community will help it to accomplish its purpose of promoting healthy pastors and congregations.

Contributors

Matthew Ackerman is a recent graduate of Calvin College with degrees in English and religion. He is currently teaching English in Budapest, Hungary, with Educational Services International. He hopes eventually to attend seminary and graduate school in linguistics and then get involved with campus ministry. Matt is a member of Family of Faith Church (CRC) in Kennewick, Washington, but is currently attending St. Columba's Scottish Presbyterian Church in Budapest. In his spare time, he likes fly-fishing, travel, and making music.

Shiao Chong is the Christian Reformed Campus Minister at York University, Toronto. He is married to Martha Schreiber and has two daughters, Alyssa (7 years) and Bethany (5 years). He attends Rehoboth Fellowship CRC in Toronto. Chong was born in Malaysia, where he converted to Christianity at the age of 14. He came to Canada initially as an international student and earned a master of arts in English literature from the University of Alberta, Edmonton, where he was introduced to the Reformed theological tradition. Chong was a contributing editor for *The Banner* for four years.

Judith Deem Dupree is the author of three volumes of poetry: *Going Home, I Sing America,* and *Living With What Remains*. In addition, she writes fiction, music, and whatever else comes to mind. She also teaches creative writing at workshops. Judith is founding director of *Ad Lib*, a Colorado-based retreat for the arts and has recently initiated a full-spectrum arts network in east San Diego County called *Mountain Empire Creative Arts*. She and her husband Richard developed QUIDDITY PRESS in order to publish occasional quality works in the Christian tradition. She lives in Pine Valley, California, and is a member of First Presbyterian Church in El Cajon, California.

Kristen Cnossen Nichols is a writer and English teacher who lives in Southern California. She grew up attending Prosper Christian Reformed Church in Falmouth, Michigan. After graduating from Dordt College in Iowa, she moved to the Los Angeles area where she earned a master of fine arts in creative writing from Antioch University. She teaches writing classes at Coastline Community College in Orange County. Her family attends Rancho Community Church in Temecula, California.

Jennifer M. Parker is a Christian freelance writer-editor, photojournalist, and teacher from Mississippi. She holds a degree from Harvard in English and American literature and language and has done postgraduate work in creative writing (Goddard College, Vermont) and education (University of Mississippi). In addition to her creative pursuits in fiction, poetry, and drama, Jennifer has served as an editor with *Urban Family*, *Reconcilers*, and *The Banner* magazines. Her articles and reviews have appeared in numerous publications. Jennifer's current post is as associate editor with AgapePress, a Christian news service based in Tupelo, Mississippi. She attends Word of Life Church, a nondenominational congregation in Tupelo, Mississippi.

Douglas A. Rottman received a degree in English from Calvin College and a master's degree from Arizona State University. After eleven years as a counselor for ADHD children and adults, he began working as a school social worker in the West Michigan area where he lives with his wife, Mary, and their three children. Doug is working on a memoir of his life to be published by FaithWalk in 2007, co-authored with his mother, Carol Rottman. He is also a member of the Christian Reformed Disability Concerns Committee. During his leisure time, Doug enjoys spending time with his family, listening to music, and visiting the beach and the Colorado mountains. Doug is a member of Plymouth Heights Christian Reformed Church in Grand Rapids, Michigan.

James Calvin Schaap was born and reared in Oostburg, Wisconsin, but for the last thirty years has lived in Sioux Center, Iowa, where he is a professor of English at Dordt College. He is the author of over twenty books, hundreds of articles and stories, film scripts, meditations, and five novels. Recent titles include the short story collections *Paternity* and *Startling Joy: Stories for the Christmas Season*. His newest works include *Crossing Over: Stories of Asian Refugee Christians* (2006), and *In His Feathers: The Journals and Letters of Sharon Bomgaars* (2006). Jim is a member of Covenant Christian Reformed Church in Sioux Center, Iowa.

Jack VandenBorn grew up on a small farm north of Edmonton, Alberta, in the 1950s. After high school, he attended the University of Alberta and attended the First Christian Reformed Church in Edmonton where he met Avlyn Ellen, married her in 1964, became a teacher, and fathered two children. Forty years later, there are three grandchildren as well. He teaches English and is the principal of a Christian school in Houston, British Columbia, surrounded by mountains, meadows, and loggers. He and Avlyn love to ski the meadows, pick huckleberries on the mountainsides, listen to (and sing) rich music, read powerful books and essays, and participate in lively church services. They are members of Houston Christian Reformed Church in Houston, British Columbia.

Michael Vander Weele teaches English at Trinity Christian College. One of his interests is the frequency with which economic images appear in John Calvin's writing. Michael suggests that the theological value of exchange might help us think of literature not so much as self-expression but as sophisticated social communication. He has written essays for *Religion & Literature, Christianity & Literature, Renascence, Nineteenth-Century Studies,* and has contributed to several book projects. He also belongs to a Christian-Muslim dialogue group that works to promote interfaith understanding. Michael attends Hope Christian Reformed Church in Oak Forest, Illinois. In his spare time, he can usually be found on a bike or in the garden, habits learned through a childhood spent in Pella, Iowa, and Waupun, Wisconsin.

Lorna Van Gilst is an English professor at Dordt College in Iowa. Previously, she taught English in Ripon, California, and served as managing editor of *Christian Educators Journal.* Lorna has taught various short-term English courses in Ukraine and in several Latin countries. In Northwest Iowa, she coordinates an English language learners volunteer tutoring program affiliated with *Amistad Cristiana,* a ministry among Hispanics. Lorna is a member of Covenant Christian Reformed Church in Sioux Center, Iowa.

CHAPTER 1

God's Voice

Kristen Cnossen Nichols

All pastors hope and pray that the words they speak, in the name of Jesus, offer strength for the season and wisdom for the journey. Perhaps more than any other, that hope abides at the heart of the motivation most young pastors carry into the profession. In this loving tribute, Kris Cnossen Nichols parses the words of the homily her pastor offered her and her husband at their wedding and then locates moments in her life when those words carried not only specific application but also abundant blessings.

I dig the video out of a box marked "Cedar Chest" in the garage cupboard. The cedar chest hasn't found its place in our new home yet, so its contents remain here—my wedding shoes, our pictures, some dried flowers, the garter. Things from later, too—sad things—my uncle's funeral bulletin, a newspaper from the day of the shuttle disaster. I take the wedding video to the VCR, push it in, and press "play."

The moments before the ceremony flash across the screen: bridesmaids in amethyst dresses, a crowd of people crammed into a small fire-lit room on a day that turned rainy at the last minute, groomsmen, our moms lighting the candles. Pastor Harold stands at the front, his Bible in his hands, my soon-to-be husband standing beside him. I come down the aisle on my father's arm. Pastor Harold begins to speak.

"I remember the first day you came to church with your parents. That day I adopted you into my life."

I didn't expect to meet a pastor like Harold Korver when I first visited Emmanuel Church in Paramount. I was new to Southern California, fresh out of Dordt College in Sioux Center, Iowa. I had grown up in rural northern Michigan; then lived in just-as-rural northwest Iowa during college. Moving to suburban LA, such an urban place, threw me into the culture shock everyone predicted it would.

My mom had driven across the country with me when I moved. We made our way across the states, driving the freeways—Interstate 80, 70, the 15—weaving our way through cities such as Des Moines, Lincoln, Denver, and Las Vegas.

Not one of these places prepared me for the crush of traffic—six lanes in both directions in some places—in Southern California. Bright sun. Glaring desert heat. A dry wind and mountains. It was all foreign.

I had accepted a teaching job in Bellflower, a city in southern Los Angeles County, where cities spill over into each other, and concrete covers almost everything. It was as different from home as any place I could ever have found. Streets were lined with strips of stores—pawn shops, real estate and insurance agencies, flower shops, sushi places, and Mexican restaurants. Windows of homes were barred. Lawns were tiny, if they existed at all, and homeless folks pushed shopping carts and dug through garbage cans, pulling out anything that could be recycled for money.

In Michigan the road my childhood home stood beside was dirt. The half mile from the main road was lined with my family's farm buildings, hay and corn fields, and woods filled with red maples, red and white pines, poplars, deer, raccoons, small ponds and cricks. The nights were quiet and dark. Two cars rarely met on the road in front of our house. If they did, we called it "traffic." I had rarely driven on a road with more than one or two lanes going in each direction. I had graduated from the Christian high school with twenty or so other people, most of whom I'd known since kindergarten. I'd never seen a person who didn't have a home.

The best way to deal with feeling completely out of place, I thought, was to try and attend a Christian Reformed or Reformed church in order to have familiarity with at least something. The drive to Emmanuel Church from my newly acquired townhouse—also a newly acquired word—took me through the rental neighborhoods of Bellflower. Homes were built one on top of the other; claustrophobic streets teemed with cars that ran the gamut—Mercedes and BMW's with shining rims, tricked out rides with hydraulics and custom paint, old beaters that barely held the road. Graffiti peeked from the corners of brick buildings and splayed across the street signs. A tall sound wall ran along the 91 Freeway up to where the cities changed from Bellflower to Paramount. There, the chain link fence featured a large hand-painted sign: "Where is our sound wall?" it asked. A man with a cardboard sign asking for help sat beside the Downey Boulevard exit, staring blankly past the cars coming down the hill to stop beside him. All of this was on the way to church, but then I had been forewarned that Emmanuel wasn't in the best of neighborhoods.

Emmanuel was known as the big church in the area, the one that pulled in lots of new Christians, and I thought it was probably more of a seeker-oriented place than I was looking for, the kind of Southern California wannabe mega-church that was more about the show than the gospel, more about the numbers attending than the authenticity of the word that was coming from its pulpit. In addition, from the looks of things, I wasn't too sure I was safe in this neighborhood I was driving through. That first morning, I was almost certain it wouldn't become my church home.

I was wrong. That first day, my mom was still there with me, no doubt worrying but being too good of a mom to say anything about it; I was young, single, and probably broadcasting my not-from-here-ness.

Pastor Harold was standing at the door. Although I don't remember his exact words, I think they went something like this. "Welcome, young lady. We're so happy to have you here. What's your name?"

By the end of our short conversation, he knew I was a displaced Midwesterner, and I knew that, almost thirty years earlier, he and his family had been the same when they arrived in Paramount. This man whose given name was the same as my father's told my mom and me that while I was away from my family, he would watch over me. He told us that he knew what it meant to drive into Paramount for the first time when you came from the place I did. For a young woman who wasn't sure that she had made the right decision to jump into this foreign concrete jungle, that was one of the most reassuring things he could have said.

"I remember the first day I saw you sitting there with this handsome man. I thought, 'Good, she has eyes.'"

Fast-forward to my third year in California.

I had met Matt, a tall, handsome man who coached varsity football at the school where I taught. He went to church with me, and like me, sat in rapt attention whenever Pastor Harold spoke. It was the way Pastor Harold stood behind the pulpit, always in a dark suit, white shirt, back straight as an arrow, silver hair combed back smartly. His sermons were filled with the reverberations of ones I'd heard as a kid, free of slang, free of self-conscious attempts to be hip or keep up with the times for the sake of pulling people.

He spoke what I thought of as "country preacher truth." Some in his congregation may have thought him quaint, but those colloquial stories took me home, if only for a few moments on a Sunday morning. He told stories of Iowa often, he repeated his pet sayings over and over, and when you listened in on the conversations of the people in his congregation you could hear hints of his messages.

Soon, Matt became a regular with me, and each week we would sit down and immediately flip open the bulletin to see who was preaching, always hoping that it would be Pastor Harold.

"I adopted you into my life."

He carries Starbursts in the pocket of his suit coat, and when he walks down the aisle after the service, he slips them into the hands of eager kids and tosses them over the heads of parents to high school kids down the row.

Somehow Matt and I often ended up unwrapping Starbursts as we stepped out of the sanctuary into the bright mid-morning California sun, feeling like kids who'd just gotten a hug from a favorite uncle, feeling like we mattered.

"God must really love this couple because he has sent lots of raindrops of mercy on them."

When I was a little girl, my parents knew a rainstorm would guarantee I would be playing outside. I spent hours in the yard or the woods wading up to the tops of my rubber boots, creating intricate river systems of draining puddles and mud. I would come home later, soaked to the skin but not realizing it, hair hanging in my face. None of that mattered though, because something about the rain made me feel quiet inside.

The day of our wedding brought torrential rains and forced us to move the ceremony inside at the last minute. We hadn't made a rainy-day plan—the coordinator told us that in all of her twelve years at Rancho Capistrano in San Juan Capistrano, a small beach town in southern Orange County, she had seen it rain only once on any weekend around April 7. This was time number two. One hundred guests packed into a small, Spanish mission-style meeting room—the only available meeting space on the convention center campus. The grassy hillside next to the pond where we were planning to have the ceremony was soaked.

I was calm. Yes, there was this change in plans. Yes, there were people who couldn't fit into the room and had to stand outside under the patio roof. Someone opened the windows so that they could hear Pastor Harold. The truth was that rainy days are few in Southern California, and I lived for them. As the rain poured down on the tile outside, we got married in that candle-lit room, and Pastor Harold blessed us with words we'll never forget.

"In life there are river people and there are box people. River people go with the flow. Box people put everything into a box. The problem is that the two tend to attract and marry each other."

It was the beginning of the wedding message, and Matt and I laughed.

Pastor Harold is famous for saying such things, and this time he was right. Matt was the river person, fine with life unscheduled. His favorite days were ones where we got in the car and drove with no goal more specific than seeing some place we'd never seen before. We grabbed food along the way when we were hungry; we ignored the clock; we got home whenever.

I was the box person. I liked things neat and was often overwhelmed by the process of making them so. If we went for a drive, I liked to know our destination, our time frame, and our goals for the day. I liked to know ahead of time how the day would work out. I only liked surprises if they were good ones.

Fast-forward again four years after we were married; our daughter Ellie was born.

"The grace, the extravagant grace of the Lord Jesus Christ be with you always."

After eighteen hours of labor and two hours of pushing, our first daughter finally arrived. She was two weeks overdue, and as we suspected, she was big—nine pounds, two ounces. Her tiny nails were long, and her purple-y skin was peeling. Her head was covered with soft, thick blond hair. When the doctor pulled her from my body she was crying. He laid her on my chest, and I talked to her through my tears.

"There you are," I said as I pushed the bloody blanket away from her cheek. "There you are."

Her dark little eyes locked on mine, and she went silent. We stared, strangers who instantly recognized each other. Oblivious to the reconstruction happening on my body, I simply wanted to look at my little girl.

The next morning I waited patiently for the nurse to bring Ellie to my room. She had been taken to the nursery so they could take her vital signs. It was all part of the morning routine, they assured me. She would get a bath and then she'd be back in my arms for the rest of the day. The nurse told me she'd be back by 8:15. By nine, I was worried, and I called the nursery to ask where she was.

"We'll send a nurse down to your room," the attendant said, but when she arrived, she was alone.

"There is something wrong with your daughter," she said. "The neonatologist is with her now, and the pediatric cardiologist has been called. You may come see her in the nursery, but she cannot come back to your room."

Shocked and silent, my husband and I followed her back to the nursery, where our daughter lay in a bassinet, wrapped tightly and sound asleep. The nurse explained that she was "dusky"—her skin had a bluish tint—and when they measured blood pressures on each of her four limbs, the difference between the pressures in her arms and legs was drastic. As she talked, I felt a sharp fear of losing my baby.

Later, the cardiologist explained the complications in Ellie's heart: her aorta would be too narrow to handle the volume of blood it needed to. She needed surgery very soon to correct the problem—delicate heart surgery. We sat, stunned. Someone would be cutting into our little girl's body and performing such a dangerous task.

"Look to God to fill the deep needs of the soul."

So this is what it felt like to be a prayer request, the ones with our names in the bulletin, a list I'd scanned myself every week, my own life continuing in its monotonous sameness while someone else's world was numb, or fearful, or painful, or dark. I'd even heard pastors run down the list in prayer, almost as if they were checking off each name as they went: her cancer, check; his father's death, check; their car accident, check, check. We had become the list of the prayed-for, and it was a lonely place.

Suddenly the sincere prayers of pastors and friends were all that we had to hold us up. Knowing other hearts were doing the best they could to share our pain was the way we knew God shared our pain too.

I pushed the button on the answering machine and leaned against the counter as I listened to the messages. I felt as if I could melt down into the floor; the exhaustion was overwhelming. My husband and I had spent yet another day at the hospital, sitting in the NICU next to Ellie and watching the nurse adjust IV's and dials, watch vitals, and prepare her for surgery.

We spent hours doing little else than staring at Ellie's pale little face and stroking her tiny hands. The skin under her fingernails was bluish, and leads attached to her chest connected her to a monitor that constantly recorded her heart rate and respirations. A small red light bulb taped to her big toe measured oxygen saturation, and I sat in a chair watching the numbers flash—96…95…93…98.

Back at home, "beep" went the answering machine.

"Hello, dear people," said a familiar voice. "This is Harold Korver. The Lord's boundless grace to you and your little Elisabeth. We are praying for you. The Lord bless you and keep you. The Lord make his face to shine upon you, be gracious to you, and grant you his peace. We love you."

I looked at Matt. Few voices were as reassuring, and, for a moment, we felt as if we weren't alone. I remembered how that spoken blessing ended every single church service when I was a girl. I'd never paid much attention to it because I heard it so many times. Now it carried weight, and I listened to the message again, felt the cadence and the age-old phrasing of the words, and Pastor Harold's voice reassuring me that God was steadfast, that he still existed somewhere in all of this.

"If you climb any family tree high enough, you'll find a few nuts. Celebrate the good things about your family."

The day of her surgery was terrifying. We signed waivers, met the anesthesiologist—she looked our age, looked as if she'd just come in to work after an early morning surf session. Matt and I couldn't decide if her appearance was comforting or scary. We sat in a waiting room surrounded by his parents, my parents, his sister, one of my best friends, his parents' best friends. We tried to drink coffee and eat scones. For some reason, Matt settled in on the couch next to his Dad, and I went over to sit on the armrest of my mom's chair. My dad was reading the newspaper. Matt's sister was grading math papers. We'd taken up residence in the in-between place where people go when something unbelievably frightening is happening and yet their hearts continue to beat and their lungs continue to breathe. I tried not to imagine what was happening, not to see a scalpel slicing layers of my baby girl's skin, her tissues; I tried not to think about the possibilities of damage, of paralysis, or worse. My body hurt in ways I never knew it could, but I didn't really notice.

Matt's dad was doing what he did best. He was telling stories. I didn't listen—I had heard most of them anyway. He never let the truth get in the way of a good story. I took comfort in the sound of his voice, in the sight of my own dad with his feet stretched out in front of him and the paper up in front of his face, in my mom's knitting needles clicking, in the feel of my friend's arm as she sat close to me.

Then, the surgeon appeared in the doorway. He was smiling.

The worst moment came later, when they moved her from recovery to the pediatric ICU. I wasn't prepared to see the anesthesiologist and the nurse racing down the hall, Ellie on the bed between them, the anesthesiologist squeezing the bag, breathing for her as they pushed her past us.

I cried for the first time. She was a bundle of wires, needles, and tubes.

When she finally opened bleary eyes and lay gazing at us, I realized it was Tuesday evening and tomorrow she would be one week old.

Early that evening, a smiling face appeared in the doorway. Pastor Harold stepped into the room. We'd had no idea he was coming, but his presence was reassuring. He laid his hands on Ellie, said the blessing again and prayed over her. He was gone as quickly as he'd appeared, but the feeling that God was there with us remained.

To our amazement she recovered quickly, was breastfeeding again soon, and went home two days early on Sunday, less than a week after her surgery.

We finally put her into the car seat, and I sat beside her, wondering what in the world I was going to do with this little creature when we got home. I had horrible fears that her aorta would break open and she would die right there in front of me once we got out of the hospital parking lot.

As we pulled up to the front of the house, we saw that our moms had painted a huge banner and hung it from our front porch. "It's a girl!" it proclaimed.

"Always grant them a holy reverence for the gift you've given them."

On Ellie's baptism day she was just over two months old. I dressed her in a little white dress with pink tulips appliquéd on the front and put a lace headband in her thick blond hair. Matt held her as Pastor Harold spoke.

"Elisabeth is truly a miracle," he said as he lifted the cover to the baptismal. He dipped his fingers in the water, then placed them on her forehead. "Elisabeth Karen Nichols, I baptize you in the name of the Father, the Son, and the Holy Spirit." Once again, he laid his hands on her, and he prayed.

"I'm reminded of a word my mother gave me
when we had the third crop failure, and it looked
like there would be nothing.
She said, "Harold, do you see that North Star over there?
You just focus on that North Star
and learn to plod, plod, plod, and keep doing the little things well."

Some nights I stood beside Ellie's crib with my hand lying on her cheek, my fingers threaded lightly into her soft hair. Most of the time she had trouble falling asleep and tossed around, needing to be soothed. It was almost as if she didn't know what would make her feel better, what would take that unsettled feeling away; but when I laid my hand on her cheek, she always put both of hers on it, turned her face into my palm and fell asleep.

What is it about the touch of a most trusted person that makes us settle like that? Is this one of the ways that we feel the touch of God, or at least the closest thing to it that we can find here on earth? I used to make my own mom stay in my room at night until I was asleep. The touch of her hand as she rubbed my back made everything fade away, made everything all right.

Ellie was colicky. Life with her began to feel like plodding. We tried to do the little things well. We tried everything, but the crying just seemed to get worse. Every night she struggled to "find her sleep," as my mom called it. We swaddled her tightly, turned her on her side, jiggled her, and shushed her. Sometimes these things worked. Other times she cried inconsolably until, exhausted, she finally dropped off to sleep. We were beside ourselves, tired out and feeling inept as parents. It seemed no North Star existed. We worried about her heart, wondering if the reoccurrence the doctors warned us about was actually happening.

At her four-month Well Baby exam, her pediatrician tried and tried to find her femoral pulses. Not being able to find them was the first clinical indication that the coarctation was returning. He sat next to her on the examination table, positioning and repositioning his fingers, trying to feel any whisper of something that would indicate the blood was pushing through the arteries the way it should. He could feel nothing, and he called the cardiologist immediately to set up an emergency appointment.

Within two days Ellie was back in the hospital, scheduled for a balloon angioplasty. Our fears had proven correct, and what had looked like colic was actually a reoccurring coarctation. When she had her original surgery, she weighed about nine pounds. Now, four months later, she had grown to sixteen pounds, and even though her body had grown so well, her aorta had not.

The doctors planned to thread a delicate catheter through her groin and up into her aorta. They would take pictures and measurements of the narrowing. If they deemed it possible, they'd inflate a tiny balloon and stretch the vessel.

On the day of the catheterization, we carried her to the cath lab where we met the anesthesiologist. Her bed was prepared—she would lie there, unconscious, in front of a wall of what looked like television monitors.

"You may hold her while I give her the medicine, if you'd like," he said. He injected a liquid into the IV line in her foot. She immediately went limp in my arms; her lips purple instantly. Gently he covered her mouth with a mask. I'm sure he could see the fear in my eyes. "Sometimes it does that to them," he said quietly. "She's okay. She just needs a little oxygen." He took her from me and put her down on the bed.

Matt put his arm around my shoulder, squeezed hard, and turned me toward the door as once again we left our little one in the hands of doctors who would attempt to perform what seemed like such a delicate miracle.

"We pray you will always give them a holy awe of your steadfast love revealed in Christ."

Ellie sat in her bath chair, kicking her feet against the side of the bathtub. She loved the hollow thumping sound her heels made. She giggled. Her Daddy was giving her a bath; he washed her hair, soaped her head up royally, and molded her hair into a sudsy Mohawk. He took a picture—one of literally over a thousand that we already had.

A month and a half since her angioplasty, her pulses beat strong whenever we checked them. We were blessed.

Before Ellie was born, we'd made the decision that so many expecting couples often make. We'd decided to stop renting and buy a house. Our search for an affordable home took us over an hour away, too far to attend Emmanuel Church regularly. We left our church home sadly, but computer technology allowed us to keep our old phone number, and we still received phone calls from the Emmanuel phone tree. We came home and found messages on the answering machine that spoke of the current sermon series, the upcoming events, and the happenings at Emmanuel. Those messages were a link to Pastor Harold and the church we loved.

One day I came home from shopping and went up to the office to check the messages. Ellie sat on my hip as I listened to Ken, Pastor Harold's son, thanking everyone for the prayers offered for his dad.

I panicked and called a friend to find out what had happened.

Pastor Harold had had a stroke. He was in the hospital.

"I can't imagine the world without him," my friend said.

Me neither. That first Sunday I drove into Paramount, I never would have expected that my life would be so strongly influenced by the simple knowledge that God's grace and a steadfast faith existed and had been offered to me in the person of Pastor Harold Korver.

"...to bless, build, and beautify..."

The Thanksgiving season arrived, and with it, a form letter from Emmanuel inviting us to the special holiday service. I scanned it quickly and noticed that Pastor Harold had jotted a note at the end. His writing was a little jagged—I couldn't help but wonder if this was an effect of the stroke. "Sure would be nice to see you and your little one at Thanksgiving," the note said.

Every Thanksgiving, Pastor Harold gets up and acknowledges all of those who have passed away and all of the babies who have been born in the previous year. He reads off the names of the departed, and the congregation sings "For All the Saints," a celebration of lives lived here and souls passed into glory. Then, he invites the parents of babies born in the previous year to bring their little ones to the front so we can celebrate their arrival. Matt and I decided Ellie should be part of this celebration.

On Thanksgiving Day, I walked to the front of church amid a crowd of other parents who were as thankful as I was to be carrying a new child. When I got up on stage, Pastor Harold gave Ellie and me a hug. His eyes told me that he was celebrating all of our miracles with us.

The congregation sang, "He's Got the Whole World in His Hands," and I couldn't sing along because I blinked away tears as I held my whole world in my hands; Ellie looked around, wide-eyed, at the other babies, at people in the congregation.

****

The tape is running low, and the ceremony on the screen is drawing to a close. The baby monitor beside me is quiet—Ellie is asleep, napping peacefully in her crib. Four and a half years have passed since our wedding, eight years since I first attended Emmanuel. It seems as if I have only blinked, and those years are gone, such a large chunk of my life.

My dad has always begun each family meal with the Lord's Prayer. The words, the rhythm of my dad's voice—it is all part of a deep ceremonial spirituality in which I was blessed to be raised and that found me again through a pastor when I moved far, far from home. When I was little, my dad's recitation of the Lord's Prayer, the way his voice lifted and fell, made me think of God. After twenty-six years of hearing my own father's lilting rendition of the words, it was only fitting that Pastor Harold finished our wedding with a blessing and the Lord's Prayer.

"...in health and in sickness, in abundance and in want,
in life and in death, abide with them that they may abide in you.
When all of life is over and their assignment here on earth is done,
may they hear you say, "Well done good and faithful servant.
You've been faithful in building and blessing your spouse,
and in pouring grace and mercy upon your children.
Enter into the mansions of the blessed.
Now teach us to pray the way Christ taught his disciples to pray saying,

'Our father who art in heaven,
Hallowed be your name.
Thy kingdom come.
Thy will be done
on earth as it is in heaven.
Give us this day our daily bread,
and forgive us our debts as we forgive our debtors.

Lead us not into temptation, but deliver us from evil.
For thine is the kingdom, and the power, and the glory forever.'
The Lord bless you and keep you.
The Lord make his face to shine upon you and be gracious to you.
The Lord lift up the light of his countenance on you and give you peace,
in your going out and in your coming in,
in your lying down and in your rising up,
in your labor and in your leisure,
in your laughter and in your tears,
until that day you come to stand before Jesus
in the land in which there is no sunset and no dawn.
The grace, the extravagant grace of the Lord Jesus Christ
be with you always. Amen."

I'm thinking that God's voice might sound a lot like that. It would be deep and rhythmic; it would recite things that were true; it would sound sincere and real; it would discard slang and lingo for the beauty of age-old words, it would persist in its presence and become part of a life.

As I watch Pastor Harold pray there on the screen, I feel this sudden urge to bow my head, reminded that here on earth, we actually can hear God's voice. Even now, Pastor Harold's words become that voice, reminding me that some people in this world are especially called and equipped to become part of our lives for a season, to touch us humbly at critical points, and to commend us into God's care.

For Further Reflection

Slowly throughout the story Nichols tells, we gain the sense, as she eventually says, that her preacher's words, miraculously enough, have become God's own voice. We might believe that, of a pastor's three-fold office of prophet, priest, and king, the office most parishioners will likely remember best—and the voice—will be the voice of the priest, as it does in the intimate stories Nichols relates. Are all of Pastor Harold's words "priestly"? Can a pastor's prophetic words become God's own voice and be memorable? What is a "kingly" voice? How might a pastor's "kingly" words become "God's own voice"?

Pastor Harold will likely be shocked to read this essay. After all, the writer pulls out an old video tape that includes words from one of dozens and dozens of weddings he's probably done in his ministry, a ceremony he may well have forgotten completely. Do you find the premise of this story intimidating? Scary? Enlightening? Confirming? Explain.

CHAPTER 2

Comfort

Michael Vander Weele

When pastors look out over their congregations on any individual Sabbath morning, they see dozens and dozens of significantly different needs. The pews—or chairs—are always full of different people, many of whom lug along completely different expectations. How does one preach to so many minds and hearts and souls? Michael Vander Weele looks back on his church life and remembers a variety of preachers from all over the political spectrum of the denomination, and concludes, finally, that the Word preached and preached well remains the most significant legacy a pastor can leave behind.

I should keep a Sunday journal, a place not so much for sermon outlines as for the ideas they have generated. It strikes me now that the best ideas I've had—too many quickly lost again—have come through agreement or disagreement with what I've heard when stationed in the pew. I'm reminded of poet Wendell Berry, who took many Sunday walks on his back forty before he had the sense to write a book of poems called Sabbaths. I don't think I have that in me, but I should at least have been collecting ideas—places where God's Word and that filament of life he's given me have met and have met with greater clarity than I usually experience. Maybe I'll begin a Sunday journal now.

Ideas aren't the whole thing, of course, but good ideas bring with them certain advantages for life. Those advantages might have been claimed better if remembered longer. I think of the sermon's role within the liturgy and of the ideas that have settled into place during its preaching. That's not all I think of though.

****

A long white banner flapped above our fifteen-foot patio. On it were the names of people from our church who had brought meals; taken our kids shopping for new school clothes; sent us on vacation; sent flowers, cards, and other forms of well-wishing; and prayed for us. The banner finally took so much ink that the names began to form constellations, not only stars. It bespoke a church as much as individuals.

We were hosting a thank you for the people who had helped pull my wife, Albertena, and our family through the stem cell transplant she had gone through in January of 1996. After her immune system and energy kicked back in, we decided to throw a thank-you party in our backyard, a late-spring, early-summer barbeque. These were the people I wanted to sit in a pew with as well as meet outside of church.

Nine, almost ten years later, we join many of these same people in the fellowship hall for the annual Christmas dinner on a Sunday evening. I don't take a hand in preparing this food, but they usually let me help serve—one of the perks for having a spouse on the activities committee. Between dinner and dessert, we gather in the sanctuary for some favorite Christmas carols. We huddle together near the back where the best sound waits to be struck, and on this night anyway, we sound almost as good as the church choir. Three weeks earlier, in this same sanctuary, our grandson was baptized and a community development missionary who works in Haiti came up to us afterward to welcome him into the church.

Much as mind and heart tell me this is what the church is all about, and much as I believe that the sermon is only part of the whole liturgy, a liturgy through which we hear God's Word and respond to it in gratitude and repentance, in my heart of hearts, I think I persevere in the pew for the same reason my father and his father did: for the sermons.

I remember coming up to my grandfather's modest home in Sheboygan, Wisconsin, usually arriving around dusk. My grandpa would be sitting in the front room, with hardly any lights on, greeting us with, "Are you here then, Edward?" To which my father would regularly reply that no, we were still on our way.

Grandpa either didn't remember the jest or never tired of it. What I do remember is my coal-shoveling grandpa carrying a *Banner* or some other church publication in his left hand, his index finger reserving the place where he had been reading. I think he most often read sermons, as if he hadn't gotten enough of them—some of which he of course disagreed with—at church. It must have been a twentieth-century, immigrant leftover from the nineteenth century's interest in reading sermons—and the *Congressional Digest*.

This is not to diminish the rest of it. I remember Harry Wierenga, in Sarnia, Ontario, foreman of my landscape crew and artist whose palette became darker as winter wore on. It was the songs, he said, that got him through the long winters. Indeed, on those few occasions where I have had to walk out of church it was because a song was so achingly beautiful that my emotion-laden head needed venting out-of-doors. Baptisms and communion services have sometimes seemed to transfigure life and made me reluctant to leave. Sometimes the written liturgy, the congregational greetings, or the singing of the choir has delivered the most important message before the sermon begins. For a while it was the prayers of an otherwise ineffective preacher that kept me returning to the pew.

Sometimes it's the people—Bob Monsma, the Pella, Iowa, rock quarry man, who bent his strong neck to the task of junior-high catechism teaching; George Alsum, the Randolph, Wisconsin, farmer who endured the loss of a teenage son in a drunk-driving accident and who told my dad that we were not called to happiness but to faithfulness—in which, after a long while, we might find some happiness still; the plumber/electrician two pews over from me who got my welder friend on a bike when he was going through a difficult divorce; the welder, who got me biking when cancer's grip on our family turned chronic; the girls' group and their leaders, who recently swooped in after adult Sunday school to host our church's AARP group for a Sunday dinner; the young people's (YEEPS) group, who have started their own tradition, hosting an adults-only Valentine's Day dinner, with Comedy Sports for entertainment. Or it's the women who seem, after years of practice, so easily to take on the tasks of nurses, or housecleaners, or advocates, or gift-givers. Woe to me if I ever separate myself from such people.

Yet, I think it's the sermon that keeps me coming back, and that against almost all odds.

Why against the odds? Because sermons can only come from people, and other people, especially people elevated above but also often dismissed from real life, can do things that are as stupid as the things I can do. Some of those things are aesthetically or psychologically stupid, but sermon-creating people can do things that are spiritually stupid too.

On the seventh or eighth day after my wife's stem-cell transplant, for example, our pastor, probably trying to be psychologically alert, didn't pray with us. He did take me out into the hall and tell me it was okay to be angry with God, even really angry with God. I knew that was true and could have heard it in a sermon on the Psalms, say, or fifteen minutes into a coffee, or over beers. As it happened I had never felt God's presence more clearly than in that hospital room and had recently finished building a small cross out of litmus paper and pipe cleaners and other hospital-room paraphernalia. What I could have used was a prayer.

A few pastors I've heard are so committed to my need to hear Jung that they neglect to tell me where God fits in—or rather, where Jung fits in with God. Some pastors can sound so religiously secure that I wonder if they have never felt the ravages of time, or of doubt; others can strive so hard to make their preaching conceptually near that it begins to sound like the personal journal of an only child. Yet, for all that, I think I stay in church primarily because of sermons.

So what is it about the sermon? Again, I need to tell a little history.

The first minister I remember—someone whose tendencies toward schism I could never have abided in a council room—had a diagonal scar that came down the left side of his face and then turned in, toward his mouth. To my young eyes, he was marked somewhat as the angel had marked Jacob's hip. I never trusted myself to take my eyes off him, except during prayer, when I could not have imagined opening my eyes before his final AMEN. In fact, the ministers of my childhood were a line of the best conservative preachers of the CRC—P. Y. De Jong, John Piersma, John De Kruyter—and much as I could not inhabit their pews easily today, I am forever thankful that I had them then.

It is out of respect for them that I say now that a good sermon is one you can learn from in agreement or disagreement. I remember Rev. Piersma, especially, telling us in catechism class not to think small—that eight (maybe it was fewer) dedicated, bright young Christian people could change the world. I remember his being light on his feet despite the fairly large body he positioned behind the pulpit, often bouncing a little on the balls of his feet, preaching the Word through his body (nothing that could be taught in a speech class).

Rev. Piersma was marked, too—not by a World War II injury but by the early death of his younger brother. When he told us from the pulpit that you had to know something about death before you could really know life, we knew this came from the deepest source within him, intermingling with God's truth. It was no surprise that he began his tenure at First Pella CRC with Lord's Day 1, "What is your only comfort in life and death?" and taught with his whole heart the Catechism's response that we are not our own but belong, both in life and in death, to our faithful Savior, Jesus Christ. Maybe it's under that banner, unfurled during the sermon, that the people in our backyard met, and all the others meet, too.

There are other advantages we can mark for sermons. I have long noticed that a middle-aged adult who stopped going to school after graduating from high school but continued going to sermons might as well receive credit for two years of college. Where else are we given such responsibilities for life-informed thought? Where else does the emphasis on *our* life outdo the emphasis on *my* life?

And sermons can model for us both the discipline and freedom of living under God's Word. One of the best examples I ever heard came from a minister in Hull, Iowa, by the name of Marvin Heyboer, whom we would chase north to hear some Sunday evenings when we lived in Orange City. Somewhere past the half-way point but before the conclusion, he would walk out from behind the pulpit and launch a five-to-seven-minute improvisation, a man with a prophetic voice talking amongst his fellow congregants, before returning to a pretty carefully scripted text. The sturdy platform he built and the dive he took off it both seemed Spirit-led, but the two different, if corresponding, discourses seemed to make incorporation of God's Word into our lives more possible, too. That was exciting!

There are so many different ways we are blessed by good sermons. We had two interim pastors recently, one of whom had a keen mother's sense of just what we had to hear, without ever sounding as if she were mothering us. The other had a sharply prophetic voice, even in retirement, that only stopped short of stridency by working its way carefully through texts. Together with God's Holy Spirit, they healed our church.

****

I wish now that I had kept a Sunday journal, a journal of analogies or corollaries that a sermon, or prayer, or song had discovered in my life. Where else but in church could I hear on the second Sunday of Advent, with news of more bombs going off in Iraq and of an older parent preparing to see her forty-something daughter die, that God's comfort means eternally righting the world—and learn, with assent, that we are called to join in that tortuous work?

It strikes me now that only through church could I hear this comfort from the son of a man who mentored me into the teaching profession and whose courses I had the bittersweet privilege of completing—it kept Ron with me longer—after he was murdered in a church parking lot in Chicago. It's Ron's son who is teaching me about comfort! As long as he can stand in the pulpit, I sure better be able to sit in the pew.

In 1997, a good friend of mine, John Terpstra, wrote something like Berry's *Sabbath* collection of poems but for indoor services. It's called *The Church Not Made with Hands,* and every pastor and liturgist (and other readers too) ought to have a copy and mark in it the inspirations of the church calendar.

Nearly a decade later, Terpstra is revisiting the subject of church. In a new chapbook just out, he writes a poem called "Needlecraft." Let me end with its words.

Before I do, however, just let me say to any ministers who may be reading these words: Yours is a sacred and vital task. God's blessings to you—also for the sake of us, your parishioners, who regularly require such blessings.

Here's Terpstra:

Needlecraft

In the church where we go to now
the words of the preacher
begin innocently enough
to thread through the fabric of our lives.
They draw together shapes
not previously recognized,
and connect portions of the narrative
as yet unread, or not yet readable,
a pattern not apparent,
as though written and stitched
by a random hand.

The church where we go to now
is, and is not, the church
of our fathers and mothers.
The old words do not come easily,
here, the songs have faded and frayed,
they have been crushed and ground
by the lives of our forebears,
the weight of history.

The preacher is not innocent.
She is both fearful and full of joy.
She would unburden us,
but the slim silver sliver that she guides
will prick
as it moves through,
and there is blood in the pattern,
the page, on the hand,
as well as healing,
just as there was for our mothers and fathers.

She pulls the thread, taut,
then snaps it between her teeth.
Amen. For now and forever

amen to this bite of a new
dispensation, ancient
and exact
as needlecraft.

(from *Brendan Luck* [Kentville, Nova Scotia: Gaspereau Press, 2005])

For Further Reflection

Vander Weele's memoirs joyfully rehearse the incalculable value of the sermon in his life. Are there moments in your life that are as memorable? Do you remember particular sermons in churches you attended? What makes those moments memorable in your life?

Schaap says in his introduction that he sometimes wonders how sermons will ever make it through our age, which is far more participatory and media-saturated. Vander Weele recounts gracious moments of church fellowship, but something in him won't let the preaching of the Word take second place to any other distinguishable feature of the church. In this age, can preaching continue to be as formative as it was in his life?

What characterizes solid and strong preaching today? Is there a difference from what may have defined good preaching a quarter century ago?

Vander Weele chooses to end his essay with "Needlecraft," a poem by John Terpstra. How does that poem describe good preaching?

CHAPTER 3

The Heart of Shepherding

Judith Deem Dupree

When pastors are introduced to others as pastors, people frequently square their shoulders righteously, as if to dress suddenly in their best behavior. While that effect may seem a professional liability, Judith Deem Dupree wants pastors to know that when ordinary people look to them for help, they are, in fact, looking for Jesus. Intimidating and impossible as that equation really is, she maintains that pastors can stand in Christ's own footsteps only by staying close to him in a very disciplined and in a very personal way.

It was an ordinary Sunday morning, like so many before it, but nothing was the same. The whole congregation knew the defeat, the soul-death of this man.

He walked slowly to the pulpit, placing each foot forward, one after the other, as if testing the ground beneath him. I could almost feel the fatigue that bowed his shoulders, that hunched them inward until he almost folded into himself. He stood before us, hidden behind the ornate podium, and my heart ached. He stood there silently, blindly, for a moment, and I wondered if *he* wondered, indeed, where he was.

Then, he offered a small, awkward smile, cleared his throat, and began, haltingly, the ancient words he knew by heart, a way through the despair, a cadence engendered from all the liturgical offerings so long practiced. This gentle man was clinging to the only hope he knew at this frightful moment: the Word—every syllable, each inflection. When he finished, silence consumed him and all of us once again.

What came to me at that moment were words I continue to hear through my many years in the pew: "If the shepherd is starving, the sheep will not be fed." That thought came to me unexpectedly, imbued with all the grace and mercy of heaven. My heart broke for him who was brokenhearted, who stood before us all with nothing left to give; I loved him, and I knew that God understood and would restore him. He did, finally.

I have never forgotten that line. It has haunted me over and over, in various situations and for varied reasons because pastoring has to be, at one and the same time, a most promising and most punishing life's work. The great hope for the church, the bedrock truth for the life's work of any pastor, and, perhaps the most intimidating realization any pastor can have is that your people are looking to you, into you, for enduring evidence of Christ.

Much of what you say and do either supports "the evidence of things hoped for" or denies it—which is why we watch you so carefully, so cautiously. Your words and deeds are the manna upon which the community of Christ feeds. Or not. The congregation *imitates* not you but the Jesus you introduce to them. Not from this alone but from the Christ you offer us is born our one true church, our community of saints, a fellowship of sinners.

Of course, no perfect church exists, no perfect congregation, and no perfect pastor. The call to the ministry does not make your individual frailties any less your particular ball and chain, even as mine are mine. Let's be honest: Sometimes all of us are deaf to the heavy clatter of our walk; we don't even know we are dragging one encumbered leg behind. When your gait is broken, however, we walk in broken step with you, or fall away.

It is the premise and promise of the Father to create, from the very mud of us, a garden—from the dust and the coagulation of your lesser dreams, a vision. Into both your fullness and your brokenness, either known or undiscerned, Christ breathes the word *Shepherd*, and into the ache of your hunger, "Feed my flock." Our great Shepherd has called your name to a particular office. It is the shepherd whom you are that I encourage, challenge, and celebrate.

We know your battle too well because we face it daily. In part, as unjust as it may seem, we want something more from you than you can ever give: We want to be shepherded, in the truest sense of the word, because eternity begins in the practice of our faith. If this eternity is not the greatest aspiration of any congregation, the fellowship does not know the meaning of the church.

But if the shepherd is starving, the sheep will not be fed. If a pastor does not strive in a fundamental and disciplined way to live in intimate relationship with Christ, the ministry will be diluted and distracted, the purposes of God depleted or defeated.

A pastor is, by practice, one who imitates Christ, in the sense that Thomas á Kempis so eloquently expressed it. It is your godly endowment—your great and sacred trust—to receive this gift of *imitation* that cannot be imitated.

The word *imitate* can best be defined in the words of Jesus, who turns and says to us all, in every situation, in his straightforward way: "…the Son can do nothing by himself; he can do only what he sees his Father doing …"

(John 5:19). This kind of imitation is that with which you were entrusted at ordination; it is the evidence we seek.

How does a pastor become—and remain—a shepherd, a doorkeeper, and a gate tender who touches that eternity we all seek? How can a pastor help an often fractious and sometimes fatuous entity such as we are to live in communion and community? It is here, in the church, where the kingdom of God is made manifest.

This, then, first: A pastor must live near unto God in order to shepherd his people. Yet, in the busyness of all of our lives, that nearness is difficult. Even pastors keep themselves at better than arm's distance, though such separation is rarely in their intent. Listen to the words of a veteran preacher.

> Pastors may not have much of a prayer life in the first place. We can sometimes believe that being busy in our profession is the same as being close to the Lord. Alternatively, we get so busy that we neglect the time for prayer. I know I constantly need to fight against this either by getting up early, setting aside the first moments of the hour in my study for personal devotions, or to remind myself that my chief work is studying, preaching, and teaching the Word, along with praying. In today's church, we can substitute programs and ministry and people for piety and personal discipline. Having a poor prayer life, pastors can be ashamed about praying or fearful their prayers will not be 'good enough'.

Many believers struggle with what it means to walk and talk intimately with God. Some believe such intimacy to be a species of naiveté, dangerous hyperspirituality, or an otherworldliness that perhaps only cloistered saints could claim to achieve. We need to be near unto him—all of us, but especially pastors. We need to be disciplined to stay in his shadow, to be Christlike in everything we do.

Some Shepherding Stories: Sue's Testimony

Many years ago Pastor Joseph called a daily early-morning prayer time at the church. He urged everyone to come and participate. My husband and I have our own quiet time early every morning and then we walk and pray together afterward. We commented to our pastor why we were not attending. He paused a moment as though "listening" in the spirit; then he said gently: "'I do not sense you are lacking in prayer.'

> This was his way of releasing us to do what we needed to do; it was settled that simply. I do not think I have ever appreciated our pastor more than in that moment. His trust in us meant so much. He is that kind of pastor; he delegates, and trusts his people

Sue's pastor saw before him a couple who had decided not to participate in a prayer meeting he knew the church needed. He might have struggled with this "rejection" by his own lay leaders, but he didn't. Their nonparticipation may seem a very small incident, but his acceptance of them became a memorable example to these two devoted servants.

This sensitivity is intrinsic to shepherding—recognizing the circumstances where people are and how those circumstances fit into the whole, then assessing them in proximity to God's love. We do not "live by sight" but by the supernatural insight God gives us.

Our faith is tested endlessly by the complexities and rigors of our lives, formidable challenges to the walk of faith. However, Jesus came to shepherd us back into abiding proximity with him. "Seek ye first the kingdom...."

All believers know his primary ground rule: Love God above all. Every pastor has learned it or heard it repeatedly for years before stepping beyond the institutional door. Staying near unto God by prayer and other spiritual disciplines is eternally vital. Of such is the kingdom.

Denise's Testimony

> Daddy lay in the hospital for eight months near death and in great pain. Pastor Mark came often, sat and listened to me and my family when we wanted to ask questions or talk. He just became God's gentle presence while we were going through it all. When Daddy died, right before Christmas, Mark was right there. He helped lead the funeral.

The pastor came and listened—the ultimate gift of quiet fidelity, a gift that confirms the presence of God among us. Of such is the kingdom.

If the kingdom of God is simply, and profoundly, recognition of who Christ is (think of Peter's persistent questioning of our Lord), it would seem that to follow him to wherever he is would be to enter kingdom territory, to enter places where pastoring truly becomes pasturing, in the sense of Psalm 23. Eyes must be opened—all of ours, not just the pastor's—because the footprints of Christ beyond the empty tomb are invisible otherwise. It is the privilege of the pastor to place one's feet in Christ's large footprints and follow those prints, over and over, through endless mazes created by the tortured digressions all of us create on the way back home to him. Our earth-nature will ever try to usurp his. In the night watches all of us keep, we all cry out to him, seeing this disparity, finding no home but his heart.

Peter received both the greatest accolades and the fiercest of rebukes from his Lord, and spoke both the eternal revelation of God and the easy cop-out of the enemy; he walked immediately in and out that door. Like him, we are each a mix of the sacred and the profane. In all of God's chosen servants there germinates the potential for both good and ill.

Every pastor is Peter, as is every parishioner, and that truth gets set aside too often. No congregation or member can demand or expect more than what God asks of his shepherd. Neither can a pastor demand more of a congregation.

Then, not less either, because what our God asks of both is a consistent resolve to live in sacred context with each other as servants of the one who became that context. Why? To breathe life into his earthen body so that we, his church, may become the recognizable community of Christ, a community that transcends all other notions and purposes of community, a community whose mission is to call the sinners home.

If we read carefully and prayerfully the astounding passage known as the Sermon on the Mount—our true roadmap—then we can see that the reality of our Lord's kingdom has always been mysterious in its utter simplicity and for that reason quite hidden from our laden hearts. As Christ gives us power, in our walking and talking with him, that sermon becomes and remains our roadmap.

It is the ongoing work of the pastor, along with lay leaders, to establish the premise that will undergird and enfold the corporate life of the congregation. That premise must be to serve His purposes, and that service will only be possible when his people—and certainly his shepherds—walk and talk daily to the Lord.

Neola's Testimony

"When the Lord first led me into ministering to pastors, I followed with much trepidation. My reaction was, 'Who am I to be doing this?' The first time God had me pray for a pastor personally, it was a man internationally known. Yes, I was intimidated. When I told this gentleman that I felt that I was supposed to pray for him, he was humbly submissive. Thereby I was encouraged.

I try to be sensitive to circumstances and the leading of the Holy Spirit, but not all pastors consider prayer, theirs or others, to be priority. I make it a practice to pray before services, especially for the service. Not all pastors appreciate that and some express resentment. I find that hard to understand in view of the Scriptures."

This strong prayer-person knows that humble, heart-felt intercession is the best of gifts lay people can give pastors. Without the ongoing, discerning prayers of your people, your vision is clouded. You are simply not called to walk alone, not called to "impart" so much as "reason together."

A pastor without a vision is rudderless, but the rudder must not be fixed in lock position. If the pastor and lay leaders, as representatives of the larger congregation, are not in general accord over church-life purposes, decisions are less apt to be a supported and grounded part of church life. Prayer for unity of purpose, and at times a short or even lengthy season of waiting upon him, is the only godly recourse.

A pastor who truly becomes a shepherd is not apt to remain a "wannabe." When the people see this truth in your witness, we all celebrate because your humble spirit invites trust at a deeper level. If they could frame it simply, your people would say this to you, over and over: "Become who you are meant to become."

How easily that idea flows from the pen and how difficult it is in execution. How ragged are all of our own garments of faith. To become who you are to become supposes that God does have a plan for our lives. Even more, it presumes that we can know that plan and walk in it.

Most of us who have walked a mile or more down the path of where we believe he wants us have experienced the *fluidity* of his plans; changes are often stunning because he shifts gears when our engines sputter, backs us up, and starts us over. Yet, we also come to treasure the way he shrugs off our incessant grasping and gasping and still loves, nonetheless, the way we hold tight to his hand.

Prayer is, of course, central. What could be more at the heart of our lives than our being near to God? We will know who is in control by your responses to crises great and small and by the way you see, or not, the eternal in the ordinary. Your delicate task, in every situation with your people, is to model the often-abnormal ways of God in such a way that they become the norm for all of us.

Darlia's Testimony

Shock settled over me like fog, consuming my world, making what was real, very unreal. My life was changed forever. My husband was gone. Until then, death was a possibility, an inevitability, but never a reality. Questions without answers bombarded my brain, haunting every thought.

> That night, where time and life seemed to stop, I looked to my pastor for guidance and wisdom so I could make the decisions others said couldn't wait. I saw his strength, felt his compassion, and heard the prayers he offered on my behalf. That is when the first stirrings of hope broke through to my spirit.
>
> A pastor who lets God's love flow through him, becomes his loving arms with skin. The Lord uses him to bring healing and hope to a world where so many are hurting. Could there ever be a higher calling or a greater sacrifice than to be God's chosen to bring comfort to his people?

We want to know that God loves us. We want to know GOD – to know HE IS. We don't come to church simply to find God, but if we don't find him there, nothing else will work. Nothing else will shatter our peripheries and gather us back together inside, into something greater than all our disparate parts.

We need you when we need him. It's that simple, that profound. A pastor is not a substitute for Christ; but a pastor can become, as Darlia recognizes, Christ's manifest love.

Carl's Testimony

> I am a writer—not well known, nor highly published—but writing is my gift from God. When the cover of my first book in nearly twenty years was completed, I took the printout to my church office to share with my pastor and staff the excitement of seeing it in living color. It simply needed to be blessed. Or, I felt it did.
>
> When I got there, I knew that I had made an error in judgment. It was not so much the words said, as the tepid response. The pastor never made reference to it again, never asked about it, but worse, to me, not long thereafter preached a sermon about the dangers of being ambitious and proud and self-focused, and so forth. He used, as the primary illustration, one of the premier Christian writers of our time, a pastor, who, in my pastor's words, was "so humble that he never told anyone in his congregation he was a writer."

As a result of his treatment, Carl learned to protect what was dearest to his heart. If, perhaps, he needed correction, those words should have been private and full of care and mercy.

Be that as it may, we will always protect ourselves until we know, bone deep, on the basis of God's love, that there is nothing of ourselves in us that needs protecting. Conversion, as all of us know, requires a dying of self before the birth of the new, and we are, all of us, still learning that death is indeed life. The transition is grace, all grace, that resurrects us over and over. It *is* a lifelong lesson that we are taught, continuously, often from the most unexpected and unlikely sources, when we are alert, or alerted. On our way, he causes us to rub elbows and souls with others who both irritate and soothe the skin of our psyches.

If our reaction to criticism, direct or implied, to backbiting, lies, and other distortions is heated—even if it is proportional to the instigating factors—we become a part of the problem, a shard of the brokenness. What believers need to see from their pastors is a response that convinces us that Christ is in control. All of us, pastors and congregations, need to be assured that if or even because we are wrong or petty or dense, we will not be dismissed—even if we are straightforwardly, respectfully, given correction—without venom and with undiminished mercy.

Where we're not wrong—either of us, pastor or parishioner—and to the extent that we are shown to be guileless or guiltless, we need to know that such evidence will be received with grace. This is the way of Jesus, who was never wrong and never wronged others by his "rightness."

Richard's Testimony

> It was the season of Easter, and I had been asked to direct a Maundy Thursday presentation involving a recreation of the Last Supper as the primary vehicle for the service. Pastor Z was a bit anxious, I think, not being in control of a service, but was cooperative in letting me put together the whole worship service, along with the acting out of the table drama, in which men depicting the disciples would, at designated times, rise and give a short speech concerning their perception of Jesus and his ministry. I wanted to bridge into the service from the congregation's preservice chatter with some appropriate music to shift the mood and decided on a tape of Samuel Barber's 'Adagio for Strings,' which I was reasonably sure was unknown to most of the people.
>
> Now, it is sometimes remarked that in the "low church" tradition there is not enough attention paid to aesthetics in worship. The congregation gave no evidence of this. As the music played, they quieted down and very evidently began to accommodate the solemnity of the preparation.

> Suddenly the pastor came up to me with some degree of urgency and asked me if he could please "make an announcement." Astonished, perplexed, and, truthfully, more than a bit irritated, I dismissed the suggestion with a quietly uttered, but decisive "no." I still find this encounter almost unbelievable. (The announcement, deferred until afterward, was hardly an emergency.)
>
> I can just see it now... Barber's "Adagio" settling into its soft, fading harmonies, followed by, "Folks, before we begin, I'd like to share this announcement with you...."
>
> "'Whatsoever things are beautiful.' Yes, but let's not let them get in the way of church news."

A small thing? Maybe, on one level, but, in the kingdom of God, there is time for everything that matters. To interrupt the flow of the Spirit *and* the dedicated creative effort that provided this segue simply for an information update would certainly diminish both.

We lose more than we realize by our inattention to what is truly happening before us in the kingdom. The Spirit is grieved. Your agenda must be quietly checked against his as you walk through the days, or you will displace or diminish him as surely as did Peter when, immediately after his identification of Jesus as the Christ, he rebuked Jesus for proclaiming his own pending death (Matt. 16:22). Peter was speaking sincerely, from his own heart. Jesus knew that. Later, in the garden, he tried to defend Jesus with his sword (John 18:10). Both reactions—denial and defense—were all-too-human responses to his deep distress. Because you are the emissary of Christ, you are not your own, and your *ways* are not yours. The shepherd does not belong to him- or herself, but then, none of us do. All of us have so much trouble remembering that.

A pastor's time is not his or her own. All but the most unperceptive of his parishioners are aware of that. There is no human way of adequately keeping abreast of all the ongoing needs—church, home, and beyond. More often than pastors would care to admit, I'm sure, they feel the weight of the world upon their shoulders.

God's shepherds need to know that their people can understand this rush. They need to know that if they are overburdened by the demands, that burden can be shared—sensitively, carefully, humbly—and that pastors can anticipate our care and concern. That burden, however, needs to be offered. None but the most needy want to wear you out; we want to bear you up as you bear us up.

Please don't play church. Don't try to be our all-in-all; that's Jesus' place. Pastors are as prone to burnout and depression as many, if not most of us. When you are weary, you probably want to pull away, and need to, to regain your vision and balance. We can probably see it in your eyes, hear it in your voice. The Holy Spirit bears witness.

Let us know—some of us, at least—that you need us as much as we need you. We will love you the more for your confession of being a weary servant.

Fleta's Testimony

> Here's what's really, really good: Ministers who are fellow travelers. The one who will invite you to watch a sunset and contemplate the beauty of God, the one who calls and says, "Your insight was so important to me that I used it in my sermon last week." The one who might just cry with frustration, joy, anguish, and pity, ministers who speak volumes just by listening.

We all know it's the deepest favor, but we'll say it anyway: your heart is all we ask of you. Without your heart in our keeping, we will know that something is amiss. Your greatest gift to your people is to care for them in all the small and great ways that matter.

> Not so good: ministers who have agendas. A while ago, when I was drowning in problems at work, in marriage, and family (notice how problems come in threes and all seem to jump on you at one time), I realized the Bible study I was leading for the youth was suffering due to my energy being pulled in lots of stressful directions. I called my minister and explained that I was "not doing well" and needed help with the study. I asked if he could help me find someone else to take over for a few weeks until the dust settled.
>
> His response was, "Well, how are you going to solve that problem?"
>
> I realized he wasn't going to help. He had enough on his plate to worry about without adding my burden to his. He didn't even want to engage in a dialogue to figure out what was beneficial for the youth because it would just require more work. I felt embarrassed for asking.
>
> I did solve the immediate problem, but the experience taught me that our pastor was not a person I could turn to for my problems. He never asked about me, about what I was thinking, feeling, going

through. He just wanted to make sure I knew it was my responsibility to handle the part of his program I had committed to do.

So I did. God was kind and provided a creative way to get the Bible study taught, and all our needs were met. Isn't that the kindness of God? I will tell you that as soon as my time of commitment was through, I resigned my position. I did not want to continue working in an environment where I felt like a lone soldier.

Feed my lambs, my sheep, he implores.

The Lord who raised pastors up to fill the pulpit will meet them at the foot of the table. When that God places his bread and fishes in our hands, we know it, gut deep; pastors who do will divide his sustenance fluently, freely, enough for all those who gather before you. After all, to put the line from that sad worship years ago in a different way: When the shepherd *has been* fed, the sheep *will not* go hungry.

Most churches and individual congregants do not truly want programs, nor do they seek to be programmed. We all want God. We all need to save ourselves from the anguish of our own ways. If we have not walked out of our own skins and into his, none of us can help each other out of our own specious foolishness, our faithlessness and despair. We need—all of us—shepherds.

God's people—all of us—recognize those who most faithfully follow him, do so by their awe. Both pastors and their people need to be awed, to be heartened by the knowledge, and the conviction that Christ has formed us and equipped us and that he is proving us, reviving us, enabling us, step after tentative step, in his way. That knowledge begins the moment when we know we are beggars lurching our way through the rubble to be there when Jesus passes by. That knowledge makes shepherds. When pastors understand their own needs and their eternal strength, when they are fed by daily coming near unto God, by the Spirit, then all their crippled retinue—and I am one—will come struggling along behind, joyfully catching up with the shepherd's uneven but persistent gait.

Only then will we come boldly, believing in you, believing that you know the way, or will find it while we worship this unseen God with you. For we all know that someday he will find us, all of us together, and he will meet us, his children, his sheep, eye to eye.

It will happen. Amen.

For Further Reflection

"The great hope for the church, the bedrock truth for the life's work of any pastor, and, perhaps the most intimidating realization any pastor can have," Dupree says, "is that your people are looking to you, into you, for enduring evidence of Christ." Is she right about that in relation to pastors? In relation to parishioners? Is it a privilege or a burden? Reflect on your own experience in the ministry to locate evidences.

Dupree quotes a pastor who claims that sometimes pastors may come to believe "that being busy in our profession is the same as being close to the Lord." Is it? Is a pastor's ability to stay near unto God simply a matter of prayer, contemplation, or meditation? Does the weekly ritual of sermon preparation provide that experience, or is more required? Consider pastors you believe to be especially close to God: How do they achieve that intimacy? Is it simply a blessing or character? Does it require discipline? To what extent does mere age and experience help in establishing intimacy with the Lord?

Consider this statement: Of all the essays in this book, Dupree's is the most fundamental. True?

CHAPTER 4

A View from a Moving Pew

Douglas A. Rottman

Dealing with the exceptional individuals in any congregation requires some exceptional care. In this helpful and thoughtful essay, Doug Rottman, who suffered through a life-threatening accident soon after his graduation from high school, reflects on the exceptional care he received in making the transition to a new way of life in a movable pew.

Before July 12, 1981, I was an average teenager, serious about my new summer job at a resort, preoccupied with girls, music, and tennis, and looking forward to starting college in the fall. All the graduation hype had convinced me that great possibilities lay ahead just for the taking, despite my unremarkable school record. I shared a swagger of invincibility with my friends and lived as though I were in charge, for better or worse, of my future. Before leaving home, I had made my peace with my two sisters and Mom and Dad and had begun a very different type of separation from my longtime friends from Okemos (Michigan) High and River Terrace Christian Reformed Church in East Lansing.

My mom remembers better than I do the special service for graduates at River Terrace in early June of that year. There were about a dozen of us high school seniors; we'd attended different schools but shared a healthy rivalry as well as camaraderie. That night we were asked to sit toward the front of the church in a group. The preacher was not the senior pastor, Al Hoksbergen, but the campus pastor, Clayton Libolt, who spoke from Job 28 on the subject, "Searching." The text begins with an analogy of searching for stone and precious metal in the depth of the earth, reminding me of adventure-filled summer vacations our family had spent in Marble, Colorado, where pure white stone is quarried from similar dark depths. The Psalm, however, moves quickly to the point about finding wisdom, also in hidden places.

My dad was sure that I hadn't been listening and hadn't heard a thing, and he told me so on the way home.

"What part did you think I should remember?" I asked, rising to his challenge. I hit my mental "rewind" button, and nearly verbatim began to play back the words the preacher had said. I even remembered parts of the litany:

Teach us to dream, to reach—
To reach for all that you have promised,
To never stop learning as long as we live.

Dad was surprised that the words had sunk in, even though I had looked inattentive as I sat there in the sanctuary. Not that I knew much about wisdom, but several ideas had indeed registered. What none of us knew that night was how important my auditory memory and learning style would become in the years that lay ahead of me.

In the Twinkling of an Eye

A month later, when a guy from Okemos invited me to spend my first weekend off work at his grandmother's cottage with other high school friends, I couldn't resist, even though it was a three-hour drive from my workplace to the small inland lake. My family was at our cottage on Lake Michigan, close to my work, eager to attend a cousin's wedding. They were also in the process of moving from East Lansing to Cleveland, Ohio, where my dad had taken a new job and my mom was to begin graduate school.

After hours of driving alone that Friday evening with only the loud music of Van Halen and Led Zepplin to keep me company, I arrived after midnight at the remote cottage. The solitary green Corvette parked outside made me realize immediately that the promised "gathering" had fallen through, and only the guy who invited me was there. A musty old cottage, the cool and overcast weather, and the absence of my best friends were a huge letdown. Sullen and sulky inside, I urged myself mentally to make the best of it.

The next morning, we drove my old Toyota to the nearest country market, got a little food, and hoped for better weather and some waterskiing the next day.

The rest is history. I skied first that Sunday morning, dismounted by diving off a single ski to avoid swimmers and a dock, and hit the rocks below at break-neck speed. That was the last moment I moved my legs or hands at will.

My parents got the call every parent dreads: "There has been an accident. . . ." I had been badly injured, was being rushed to the nearest trauma center, and might in fact die from my injuries. They were able to find a small plane to take them across the state to Saginaw so they could be at my side.

My mother remembers every moment that happened next in images that will likely be with her as long as she lives—her only son, no longer a child, attached to machines and hardly able to speak, lying immobile on white, sterile sheets. A few minutes later, she says, she and my father reluctantly left my bedside and stumbled down a long brown-tiled corridor toward a waiting room where they collapsed on a couch and tried to hang on.

Time passed—how much, they don't remember—but the next thing she knew, a dark figure touched her gently on the shoulder—man in a brown robe with a cross dangling from his neck.

"I understand your son is in the trauma unit," he said softly. "God understands the pain a mother must endure when something happens to her son. The Virgin Mary knew the same pain you are facing today."

"Thank you, Father," she managed to say, and he took her hand. Only at that moment did she realize, she says, that St. Mary's was a Catholic hospital.

The next morning, my parents were told that my spinal cord had been severed, but that the doctors were confident I could eventually be weaned from the respirator to breathe on my own. My chances of ever walking again were, the doctors said, less than three chances out of one hundred.

Who Can Help?

Meanwhile, Rev. Al Hoksbergen had started driving west for his vacation. Because our family was moving, we had already said our goodbyes personally and at several farewell events. I had known no other pastor in my life, and I knew my family would miss this man. We knew Rev. Al as a friend, our pastor as a regular guy. His style and contemporary sermons seemed relevant to my adolescent experience and often grabbed my attention.

As much as they might have wanted to spare him the news of my accident, my parents could not, and his response was swift. He drove all night back to East Lansing, dropped off his family, and continued two more hours to the trauma center in Saginaw. Our pastor, the one who always spoke about God's presence in times of need, was there beside us. Never preachy or glib about the will of God, he simply became God's closeness to us.

Because he was "a man of the cloth" he was one of the few people allowed to come with my family into the intensive care. My little sister, then 14, remembers that Pastor Al's presence made her wonder if I was worried about "how good a Christian I was"—just in case I might die. All I knew, honestly, was that pastors come in times of trouble, serious trouble. That much I understood.

For the next three days, Pastor Al took care of all of us. He reminded my parents about the kind of a kid I was—friendly, gentle, and intuitive. "Those things don't change." He told stories, reminding them of the time when, at the groundbreaking ceremony for the River Terrace Church, I had been the first kid to respond when he asked the congregation if anyone else would like to scoop some dirt to help dig the hole. The shovel seemed huge, but I was only five years old.

I survived the accident and the regimen of hospital treatment, but there were times when all of us wondered if my surviving was really a blessing. Five days after the accident, we knew that the process of recovery and rehabilitation would take a very long time. Rev. Al took part in the decision to move me by air ambulance to Cleveland where my family would be making their home. Everyone around me was quite certain it was the right thing to do, but I wondered how Rev. Al would be able to visit after the move.

The Year Ahead: Acute Care to Rehab

Because I was not yet eighteen, the Pediatric Intensive Care Unit (PICU) of Rainbow Babies and Children's Hospital became my new home. Twelve beds, most of them cribs, surrounded me, but lying flat on my back I could hear more than I could see.

I had visitors, some of which I wish I'd never seen.

"Don't let them *ever* come in here again!" I told my mother when she came to visit one Sunday. My voice, now weakened by a tracheotomy, was barely capable of getting out the story. As I lay immobile in my bed, unable to communicate, two strangers had come the night before and prayed long and hard over me for healing, even anointed me with oil. My voice was so weak I couldn't even tell them to go away.

We were new in Cleveland, had no church home, but my story had spread quickly and I wondered if, out of desperation, my parents had asked these men to intercede.

I told my mother what I'd gone through. "It was so awful; I felt so helpless. They didn't try to talk to me—they just talked to God," I said, my voice, I'm sure, barely audible, but my anger clear. "They asked God to make me get up and walk!" I remember a tear that I could not wipe away.

Pastor George Vander Weit helped all of us through the incident and aided my parents' transition into the fellowship at East Side CRC. Before coming to visit me, he asked my parents a lot of questions—not about the accident but about me: "What kind of a guy is he? What were his dreams? Had I been serious about my faith before the accident?" As a parent of several active teenagers himself, he knew their preoccupations and could imagine my own search for independence.

He carried his well-worn Bible under his arm as Mom introduced us, but I think he was a little nervous when he came to my hospital room for the first time. She remembers hanging back and then finally leaving so that we could get to know each other better. Soon enough he adjusted to my feeble voice.

Not long after, my mom came back into my room and found Pastor George under the bed. I was on a bed called a Stryker Frame, a bed whose mattress could be turned completely over so nurses would not have to move me and disturb the traction on my spinal column. He was under it—our new preacher. His Bible had nearly fallen onto the floor when the bed was flipped, but he was unfazed and continued to chat with me from below the bed.

Before he left, he asked what kind of food I liked. I had been fed only through a feeding tube for too many weeks; television commercials for hamburgers and junk food made my stomach ache. "Bugles are my favorite," I told him. "I haven't had any for weeks!"

Every week of my hospitalization, for an entire year, I could count on Pastor George's making a visit—with his Bible and a box of Bugles.

Coming Home

Eventually, I was allowed to come home for overnight visits. In my condition, of course, I couldn't live in just any home. I remember all of us marveling that the house my parents had bought even before I was injured had only one small step at the entrance and even a first-floor bedroom.

Pastor George had thought about some of my needs even before my parents had. He'd found a ramp someone was getting rid of and pulled together a crew to install it and a hospital bed before my homecoming.

Between weekly visits, Pastor George was hatching another plan. Right down the street from East Side CRC in Warrensville Heights, Ohio, was the Thistledown Race Track. Because he was active in the greater community, Pastor George decided to pull in some favors wherever he could on my behalf. One Saturday he got an EMS vehicle to pick me up from the hospital and bring me to Thistledown.

I had never been at a racetrack before, and, if the truth be known, I doubt that George had either. However, he knew people who could alter the shape of things down at the track—who could designate one race, "The Doug Rottman Special," which they did. He made sure I could see that race and even get into the winner's circle.

Today, I treasure the photograph taken of me with the winning horse, the winning jockey, and the winning pastor.

Occasionally, Rev. Al would drive down to Cleveland, sometimes bringing along some of my old friends. On one of those visits, he learned that my most urgent need was a van with a lift. Within a few weeks, he let us know that the River Terrace Church had begun "Doug's Van Fund," and were planning fundraisers to make sure that by the time I got out of the hospital I would have wheels.

I was really still just a kid, but I'd begun to realize—and I know it even better now, years later—how many people cared enough about my life to both pray for and work toward my healing in any way they could.

Reentry to Community

With the fund, my parents were able to purchase an older van that had been used to transport disabled students at Kent State University—affordable but not in top condition. Pastor George enlisted an elderly mechanic from our church, who took on the van as his personal service. All the while we owned the van, and well into my first year at college, our van's personal mechanic, a man also named George, was ready to tune it up, even on weekends.

My dreams came back to life with that old blue van. As winter turned to spring, I longed to be out of rehab and began to think about college. I had never learned to brush my teeth or shave myself, but I had learned to use a computer and an adapted tape recorder to accomplish my schoolwork. Even though the rehab staff at the hospital urged me to go to Kent or Ohio State, campuses fully equipped for people in wheelchairs, I wanted to go to Calvin College, where I'd planned to go before all this had happened.

The Calvin campus was not set up for someone like me, but Tom Hoeksema, handicap coordinator at the college, moved quickly to convince the powers that held the purse strings to accommodate me, including remodeling a dorm suite and finding a couple of guys to live with me as my attendants, in exchange for room and board.

My first wheelchair experience in crowds was attending church again after a year away, and it was not easy. Those folks who had so faithfully prayed for me now had to deal with me in person, and I with them. Pastor George made it easier than I expected, treating me little differently than others and not making the event more of a spectacle than my electric wheelchair already did. A nurse in the congregation quietly provided me with a computer to take to college.

After several semesters at school, I decided I was ready to make my profession of faith.

"Do you intend to faithfully live for him?" Pastor George asked.

"I do, God helping me," I said.

The congregation echoed those words, but, honestly, I still wasn't sure I could make it though college or the rest of my life. What I did know, for sure, was the source of my help and comfort.

College and Beyond

Four years later, I did graduate and decided to try a warm climate, and more independence, at Arizona State University in Tempe, Arizona. Two years later, with an MSW in hand, I returned to Michigan to look for a job. I posted an ad at Calvin for personal-care attendants. A pretty blond nursing student applied and was hired on the spot. Mary was quick and efficient but often stayed longer than the work dictated. A year later, Pastor George officiated at our wedding in Visalia, California.

When Mary and I searched for a church, we found Plymouth Heights CRC, which had an elevator, making both floors accessible. When the pastors asked what the church could do for us, I admitted that I didn't like to sit in the back of the sanctuary. I don't know what happened behind the scenes, but soon two pews had been shortened, leaving a space for my chair half way down the aisle.

Like so many others with disabilities, I am at my Sunday best at worship—presentable in the crowd and surrounded by my similarly polished family. If that is the only snapshot people have of me, or anyone, with a permanent disability, it is, at best, a fragment of my life, not enough to understand what goes on, day to day, in my life. It would be a good experience for others to take a walk in my shoes—or the shoes of various others with disabilities.

Tom Hoeksema has offered something of that experience to faculty at Calvin College: one day of using wheelchairs or canes. Perhaps he saw the need, based on some of his early experiences with me in 1982: bumpy walkways, the sudden unopenable door, and classes in rooms unavailable to someone in a chair. I'd like to propose, in fact, that the experience last for twenty-four hours. How does someone actually get up and out in order to join "the thronging worshipers"? If simulation is impractical, mental "shoe wearing" can go a long way.

Going the Extra Mile

This I know: Over the years, pastors have been there for me but also for my parents and sisters and now for my wife and children. My accident created a crisis of faith for all of us, from the initial realization that nothing would ever be the same, to the day-after-day challenges of life. Reverend Al's presence within hours of the accident reminded us all that God, through his substitutes, is always present, and so it has been for over twenty years.

Sometimes I listen to my own mental tape of the words I heard in church as a high school senior, in a service my dad thought I'd not even heard.

LET US GIVE THANKS BEFORE GOD…
Grads: For changes, for new responsibilities
And for new possibilities, we give thanks, O Lord.
AND TEACH US TO DREAM, TO READ
TO REACH FOR ALL THAT YOU HAVE PROMISED,
TO NEVER STOP LEARNING AS LONG AS WE LIVE…
TEACH US YOUR WILL
SO THAT OUR LIVES MAY BE STRAIGHT AND SURE,
IN YOUR GRACE. AMEN

None of us ever know which of God's words, spoken by the minister, recited in liturgy, or sung in hymn or choruses will eventually and permanently hang in our consciousness, ready to speak to us in our weakness.

I was never as in-charge or as invincible as I thought I was at seventeen. However, the one who is in charge continues to challenge me, just as I am, with possibilities. From week to week, I hear those challenges from the pulpit, from preachers who speak in God's name, while I'm sitting in my movable pew in the middle of the church. I feel the challenge when all our hands reach out in faith and act on behalf of others who need to know, in very concrete ways, that God will never leave them.

In the quarter-century that has now passed since the accident, I've come to understand, ever more fully, that compassion and preaching go hand in hand. It is the pastor's hands and feet that make the truth of the preached Word come alive. A pastor's engagement in the everyday lives of people, all of the people, saves theological reflection from disintegrating into useless dust.

When a *real* person speaks from behind the pulpit, then God speaks mightily to real people—all of them—in the pew.

For Further Reflection

Rottman says that Pastor George came to the hospital frequently "with his Bible and a box of Bugles." Recount incidents from your own life when "a box of Bugles" was its own precious form of ministry.

Is it possible for a congregation to learn some things about its "exceptional" members by walking in their shoes? Rottman mentions a program at Calvin—can churches teach empathy in that way? What can congregations do to integrate members who have special needs?

Interestingly, Rottman remembers his first visit in church after the accident and recounts the fact that Pastor George seemed to play down that moment, "not making the event more of a spectacle than my electric wheelchair already did." How can a pastor know when enough is enough and too much is too much?

During the most difficult period of his life, Rottman's deep appreciation grew for the work of two pastors whose sheer perseverance was a testimony to God's love. That those continuing visits were important to him is obvious. Can such visits—over and over and over again—be a blessing to pastors as well? How so?

CHAPTER 5

Pastors as Mentors: Growing Leaders through Relationships

Shiao Chong

Shiao Chong admits that his becoming a campus pastor and leader in his own congregation today is something of a surprise, in part because he wasn't even reared as a Christian believer. When he looks back on the path of his life, it's impossible for him not to notice the nurturing witness of two pastors—very different men—who nonetheless shaped him into becoming what he is. His story—and theirs—helps us all understand how pastors can carry out one of the important tasks of the ministry: creating leaders.

"At its heart mentoring is about relationship."
– Walter C. Wright, *Mentoring: The Promise of Relational Leadership*

As a campus chaplain, I do more than simply pastoral counseling. I see the identification and nurture of future leaders for God's kingdom as a core part of my ministry. After all, like it or not, universities and colleges are the incubators of tomorrow's leaders. I can't say that I excel in "growing leaders," at least not yet, but I try my best.

Part of the reason I focus on leadership development is my own personal history of having been "developed"—and I'm still developing—as a leader. As a campus chaplain, albeit a currently, nonordained chaplain (hence, my inclusion among the contributors of this volume), I am a leader among the Christian community on the York University campus in Toronto, Ontario. Through written and oral presentations, I give leadership and offer some teaching in diverse matters relevant to the greater Christian Reformed Church and the wider Christian community.

I wasn't born a leader. I would not classify myself as someone who God has gifted in leadership abilities or charisma. I believe, however, that we are all called to exercise good, Christian, servant leadership when we need to, even though we may not all be gifted leaders.

So, how did I grow as a leader? What aided me or guided me into the leadership role that I have now? Two pastors from very different worlds were key to my growth as a leader, and these words are my reflections on some of the key dimensions in our relationships that contributed to my own personal growth. What I'm about to say is not meant as a how-to manual to develop leaders in some mechanistic fashion, but there are recurring patterns that I have identified as being helpful in the progress of grooming potential leaders. It seems to me that all pastors are called, similarly, to nurture leaders. I'm not alone.

Let me begin with a little personal history to give this reflection some context.

A Tale of Two Countries and Two Pastors

I was born and raised in Malaysia, a country in Southeast Asia, and I am part of the Chinese Diaspora around the world. My parents were nominally religious in the eclectic mix of Buddhism, Taoism, and Confucianism that is typical among the Chinese community in Southeast Asia. At one point in my young life, one of my older brothers—I was the youngest—became a Christian and started attending the local Plymouth Brethren church that was close to our home. Truth be said, it was the only Protestant church in my hometown at the time; the other church was Catholic. In any case, at around the age of 10, my brother, who is now a Reformed Presbyterian minister, started taking me to church with him—with my parents' permission.

I went to Sunday school. I learned the Bible stories—about Israel, about Jesus, and about God. After a year or so, I started attending worship services too. Even after my brother graduated from high school and went to university in the city, I continued attending Sunday school and the worship services every Sunday. At the age of 14, I consciously committed my life to following Jesus Christ as my Lord and Savior. Evangelicals would say, I was "born again" at that point.

Pastor Lim Fong Jwong, who was also Chinese, was the pastor and live-in janitor/caretaker of this small church (the largest membership in my memory was probably around fifty people) in a town back then of over ten thousand. "Uncle Lim," as the Sunday school children used to call him, was a clean-shaven, rotund person with a jovial personality and round-rimmed eyeglasses.

As a 10 year old, when I first met him, he looked like a jolly fat guy, who would have made a great Santa Claus, except he certainly would not have allowed any of that pagan consumerism to tarnish the religious celebration of Christmas. As I grew older, I either realized he was not as fat as I had perceived him at age 10, or else, maybe, he had lost weight. Whatever the case, Pastor Lim still had a good sense of humor.

He was my first pastor, and he proved seminal in my spiritual journey and growth as a leader. He was not a man without his faults, of course. He may well have been a tad legalistic, but, as you will see, he made a significant impact on my leadership growth.

For a Plymouth Brethren pastor, he was somewhat unorthodox. Pastor Lim held to the typical Brethren practices of keeping women silent in the worship service; of having a nonliturgical, nonplanned impromptu worship where only men were allowed to freely choose and read and/or expound a Scripture text or choose a hymn for communal singing; and of serving the Lord's Supper practically every Sunday. The services, by the way, were all in English, thanks to the British colonial legacy.

Theologically, Lim was a Calvinist and an admirer of the works of John Calvin, of the seventeenth- and eighteenth-century Puritans, and of the nineteenth-century Princeton theologians such as Charles Hodge and B. B. Warfield. Such doctrinal leanings showed in his preaching.

Lim would preach "expository sermons," in which he would explain the meaning of a text as if he were a biblical scholar writing a commentary. It made no difference if his audience was full of youngsters like myself, who may have found such intellectual stuff boring. Furthermore, Lim frequently taught the "doctrines of grace"—the catch phrase for the Reformed or Calvinist teachings on salvation by God's grace alone.

Honestly, I never found his sermons boring. To the contrary, my young mind found his rational, logical, common sense approach interesting, if not fascinating. His preaching made the Scriptures come alive for me; the texts began to make sense, and a growing awareness of a cohesive system of beliefs increasingly dawned on me as I listened attentively Sunday after Sunday.

Today, I am certain that I learned part of my preaching skills through those many Sundays of listening to Lim preach. My theological mind was being honed through those sermons and the many Calvinist theological books in Lim's library that I later devoured.

From tropical hot Muslim Malaysia, I traveled to the frozen prairie of northern Alberta, Canada. As with so many of my Malaysian peers, I became an international student at a foreign university. Having used the English language extensively, especially at church, I adjusted quickly to my new cultural surroundings. Culture shock felt more like a mild surprise for me. Such acculturation did not mean, however, that I did not suffer from homesickness and even depression during my days at the University of Alberta in Edmonton.

Prior to those dark days, however, I was immersing myself into Western and specifically Canadian culture. I studied English literature, which was my major, and I dove into the seminal texts that had shaped Western and Anglo-American culture. My favorites were the sixteenth- and seventeenth-century English writers, who were steeped in biblical and classical references.

Early on, I immersed myself into Canadian culture in another way: I watched hockey. I quickly learned, and my Canadian colleagues were eager to teach me, how to watch, to understand, and to enjoy the game of ice hockey as the hometown Edmonton Oilers marched to their fifth Stanley Cup.

Despite these immersions, I did not feel "at home" in Canada, in part because I was spiritually restless, stopping at Alliance and Baptist churches (including Chinese and Caucasian congregations), along my spiritual travels. In the classroom, my engagements with postmodernity via literary theory challenged my hitherto neatly packaged, rationalistic, systematized, black-and-white Christian faith. As the questions began to outnumber the answers, my sense of spiritual homelessness grew. Homesickness set in, and the cumulative effect drove me to a mild depression.

It was around this time that the second pastor came into my life: Rev. Tom Oosterhuis (Dutch, not Chinese), the Christian Reformed chaplain at the university.

Like Lim, Tom also makes a good Santa Claus, complete with a white beard and an excellent sense of humor. Unlike Lim, he probably would don the red suit if asked; at least, he would probably do the Dutch Sinter Klaas version. Although he shaved his beard once in a while, the bearded Tom is, for me, the quintessential Tom. Tom, however, didn't look like a "jolly fat guy"; rather, he looked more wise than jolly.

Tom was a biblical scholar—his Ph.D. thesis was on Romans—and a theologian. He taught more by prodding and provoking with questions than by simply giving the answers. He was always available, open for any question I had—no matter how blasphemous what I said might sound. In fact, he occasionally took some delight in playing the Devil's advocate. He liked to tease folks in a good-natured way, which I was told is a Dutch trait.

After a few initial meetings with Tom, our friendship grew, and my visits to his office increased. I poured all my questions out at Tom, and he took them with honesty and humility; gradually the questions in my life began to dwindle. His friendship, along with others, helped to draw me out of my depression. Eventually, I became a regular fixture at the Chaplains' Centre, participating in and contributing to the programs.

Through Tom, I learned "the Reformed world-and-life view," I discovered Abraham Kuyper and Herman Dooyeweerd, the integration of faith and learning, and the lordship of Christ in all areas of life. Through Tom's ministry, I also found a community of students who were exploring the same questions as I was. Slowly and gradually, my spiritual restlessness turned into a resting, and I found a home in the Christian Reformed Church.

I also found a home in campus ministry as a profession.

Those two pastors have been central to my growth as a believer and even my profession today—a campus pastor. When I consider the roles those two pastors played in my life, specifically with regard to developing leadership in someone who never felt he had such potential, I'd like to offer five strong themes: (1) getting along, (2) reciprocity, (3) sharing visions and dreams, (4) modeling, and (5) giving responsibilities.

Getting Along

There's a saying in leadership circles: "People won't *go* along with you if they can't *get* along with you." There's much truth in this saying. Relationships are the foundation of leadership. It's at the heart of the mentoring process. Looking back, I find that I got along famously with both Lim and Tom.

Lim was, of course, the much older pastor, and I was little more than a kid when I was in his congregation, but we gradually got to know each other in ways that outgrew any kind of hierarchical relationship. Lim enjoyed playing badminton in the church parking lot with the youngsters. He also shared my love for chess. Many afternoons, I would go to his home and play chess with him. During those games, we didn't talk much about God's sovereignty or election but focused instead on Kasparov and discovered checks.

At the time, however, I remember feeling—even then—that he treated me as an equal. He never patronized or belittled me, never humored me as if I were a child or youth. We sat over the chessboard, playing as equals.

His acceptance of me as a friend and equal spilled over even doctrinal and theological matters. When we did talk about doctrine, Lim would speak to me as if I were one of his adult church members. He would explain and prove his theological points to me, and in that way he gained my compliance, not by grandstanding or asserting authority. I felt respected. In turn, I respected and trusted Lim, not only as a pastor but also as a friend.

The same can be said for my relationship with Tom. We joked and teased each other. We dialogued and discussed everything from heavy theological and philosophical issues to light-hearted topics such as Edmonton Oilers hockey. We played pool, and we prayed together.

His hospitality was immense. He opened his home not only for socials and parties but also for accommodation; I boarded with him for a year. His family, his wife Alyce and his children Matt and Michelle, was also instrumental in my development. Tom opened his life to me.

I did not feel patronized or dehumanized into a "project" or an "object" of either of their ministries. I felt respected and loved as a person by both of them.

Reciprocity

The key to the development of friendship is reciprocity. There needs to be mutuality in relationships, a clear ability to give-and-take. Although Tom and Lim were my mentors, in neither case was our relationship one-way or top-down. Intellectual fertilization and feedback flowed in both directions.

Tom, especially, would not only welcome my thoughts and feedback but, at times, intentionally ask for it. Often, he would share drafts of his articles or speeches or even the sermons he was working on, always welcoming my thoughts and comments.

There were also things and favors that I could do for him: opening up the Chaplain's Centre on those mornings when he would be late because of an off-campus appointment, for instance. It was clear to me that he cherished and valued my thoughts, my contributions, and my help. I felt that I was needed because I thought I was. I wasn't just a ministry recipient who is there to receive charity and to have ministry "done" to him. I was a valuable member of the community, and I gave as much as I received.

I was only a youth of 14 when I became a Christian. Perhaps this reciprocal aspect of leadership training did not occur as greatly with Lim's mentoring, but that is probably to be expected. I remember, when I was still a teenager, that Lim asked me for my perceptions of a ministry intern who had been in our church for a few months and had worked hard with the youth group. Simply by his well-meant question, I felt empowered.

I had also started attending Lim's weekly Bible study at this point, the youngest attendee. I was treated as one of the adults; my replies and thoughts to the questions posed were heard sincerely, and he appreciated the engagement.

Sharing Visions and Dreams

John Maxwell wrote: "All good leaders have a dream. All great leaders share their dream with others who can help them make it a reality" (*Equipping 101*, p. 60). Tom and Lim never sat me down and gave me a lecture that began with, "This is my vision, this is my dream...." They shared their visions and dreams in more subtle ways—in the ideas and activities they chose to emphasize, in the books they chose to push, in the projects they hoped to pull off. In their teaching and speaking, listeners got a clear picture of their visions for ministry or for life. What these guys were passionate about was no secret, either to me or anyone else who spent time with them.

As a young man, I knew that Lim's passion lay in preaching, in correct doctrine, and in accurate exegesis of the Bible. Tom's passions were clearly the Reformed world-and-life view of Creation, Fall, and Redemption, the integration of faith with all of life, the lordship of Christ, as well as proper biblical exegesis. Those passions were embodied in their ministries, in their priorities, in who they were—and are—as pastors. They consistently taught, acted, and lived out of their deeply held beliefs. Whether it was a sermon or some discussion group on faith and technology, both pastors shared passionate dreams and passed them along to others who participated.

Modeling

I saw both Lim and Tom in action, up close, and those moments were important training sessions for my ministry today. Imitation may be the finest form of flattery, but, during the Renaissance, imitation was also seen as a necessary form of learning, especially in the areas of writing and speech. I did not catalog a list of dos and don'ts from observing these two pastors in action. Rather, certain moments of ministry simply got stuck in my mind as paradigmatic lessons.

Once, when only Lim and I were present for the weekly Bible study, I assumed we would cancel the session, but he conducted the study with the same zeal and quality as if a crowd had packed the room. I never forgot that, in part because I felt valued. Today, I have the same philosophy in ministry. I provide the same quality programming or presentation regardless if whether the room holds one or one hundred.

However, I try to be flexible in my programming. I remember when Tom was leading a discussion and a tangential topic arose. The group was obviously more interested in the tangent than in the topic being presented. Tom went with the flow, and we probably had one of our best discussions ever.

From that moment, I learned that people are more important than programs, that the participant's agenda is probably more important than the leader's. I have similarly "gone with the flow" in my own group discussions, especially when the group is small. Answering questions is more important than finishing off whatever it was I'd preplanned.

Giving Responsibilities

I was still a teenager, about 17 or 18, if memory serves me right, when Pastor Lim asked me to lead his weekly Bible study. He had to be out of town that week and needed someone to lead the study in his place. I was surprised when he asked me, and even somewhat surprised when I told him I would. There were, after all, adults in the study group who, in my view, could do a better job of leading. One of those regular attendees was even a schoolteacher. However, Lim must have seen something in me and felt that I needed an opportunity. He equipped me with his commentaries and pretty much gave me my freedom. I am not sure how well I did, especially in the eyes of the older adults; but I will never forget being given what seemed to me to be a great responsibility at a very young age. That was my first step, my first taste of church ministry work.

By the time I met Tom, I was more confident in volunteering and doing ministry. Having already been a devotional leader previously for a Chinese Christian fellowship group on campus, a fellowship in which I'd led Bible studies, I was more confident when Tom entrusted me to run, in his absence, one of his weekly supper-and-discussion gatherings. Cooking the meal—chicken noodle soup, as I remember—for a crowd was more nerve-wracking than leading the discussion after supper that night, but I valued the responsibility given.

One more responsibility or opportunity that Tom gave me, which I must mention, was the newsletter. He published a monthly newsletter, *Eikon* (Greek for *image* or *icon*), and encouraged students to be the editors and to write articles. Eventually, I became one of its editors.

Writing for *Eikon* gave me confidence in my writing abilities. I can't say that everything I wrote for the newsletter was great or even good, but my work on that newsletter was a first step toward writing for the public. I honed my skills of writing for a popular audience in those years.

One day, *The Banner* (the Christian Reformed Church's denominational magazine) had a contest for its readers: Write an essay on the relevance of theology. I am certain that I would not have had the courage to enter that contest if I had not already had the experience of writing for Tom's newsletter all those years prior. I was a graduate student by that time, doing my masters in English literature.

Writing for academia and writing for a popular audience, however, are two different beasts. From Tom, I got the heart to enter the contest, and, along with three other contestants, was eventually rewarded with publication.

That essay was to be the first of many more articles for *The Banner*, and other Christian publications. I know that if it hadn't been for the opportunity Tom gave me—and his urgings—I probably wouldn't be writing these words right now. My writing ministry may never have taken off.

One of the most important steps in growing leaders, to my knowledge, is giving responsibilities. Potential leaders need to be given opportunities to lead, to do ministry, as I was.

Developing Leaders

So what is there to say to pastors who seek to nurture their congregations into effective leadership?

- Get along with your potential leaders, so that they may go along with you.
- Take from them as much or more than you give.
- Share your dreams and visions, your passions in life, so they may catch those dreams themselves.
- Model your best for them to observe and even imitate.
- Give them responsibilities, opportunities, and freedom to succeed.

I learned as much from two very different pastors from two very different worlds in two very different ministries. I owe my thanks—temporal and eternal—to them both.

For Further Reflection

It's fair to say that the two pastors Chong describes in his essay are quite different from each other not only in place and time but also in the way they see the faith. Both are Reformed, but their orientation to doctrine and their basic modus operandi might well put them at odds in meetings of some mutual classis both might be part of. Nevertheless, what basic characteristics did they share in their influence in Chong's life? Do you think it's easier for some pastors to display those characteristics than others?

To what extent is it every pastor's role to mentor people? Are pastors full-time mentors? In both situations, Chong had significant personal time with the pastors he describes. Is that kind of personal time required for successful mentoring? If it is, doesn't the range of requirements of full-time ministry simply make that kind of one-on-one mentoring impossible? Where is mentoring on your own daily list of things to do? Should it be higher?

CHAPTER 6

Perseverance in Serving Up the Word

Lorna Van Gilst

Most people would call Billy Graham a "preacher," not a pastor. We might well do likewise with, say, Charles Spurgeon or Jonathan Edwards or Billy Sunday. All of them seem to us to be preachers, first and foremost. Have times changed? Lorna Van Gilst says she tells her writing students not to "preach" when they write. Perhaps the word preach—and preaching and even preacher—have suffered. In her essay, Lorna tells stories from her own life with pastors/preachers, stories that may help us to understand why we use the words we do.

Our preacher started his Family of God series the first week in September, I remember. The sermon—it was a Sunday night—charged fathers to "train up a child in the way he should go." Mothers, he said, would get their turn the next week.

A week later, he reminded mothers how to be "wives of noble character whose children would arise and call them blessed."

The third Sunday, still on task, he admonished the children to obey their mothers and fathers, whether they were still living at home with their parents or not—a sermon for everybody, he said, because we are all children, and "a wise son heeds his father's instruction." However, several of the widowed members had already decided to worship elsewhere on Sunday evenings, I'd heard, at least until the family series ended.

Perhaps too boldly, several young adult friends and I invited the preacher and his wife to visit in our home after the evening service. "Pastor," we said when the coffee was served, "you have focused on strong fathers, on godly mothers, on obedient children. When are you going to address the role of individuals in the body of believers?"

"It's not part of the series," he said quickly. "There's nothing in the Bible about singles in the church—if you can find the text, I'll preach the sermon. But God works in families."

"Of course, there's Paul," the pastor's wife said meekly.

"Not part of the series!" he spluttered. "Not part of the series!"

The series ended the next week with a sermon on godly grandparents.

In October, the widows came back on Sunday nights, and the preacher added a new petition to his congregational prayers: "Bless all the people who are single and lonely."

Stiff and often seemingly uncompromising, the preacher—my preacher—seemed to take his marching orders only from God. If a matter or a question wasn't addressed in the Scripture, he simply assumed he didn't have to have an opinion—or a sermon. As a single person, I felt left out of the fellowship. We all did.

The problem was that our preacher had always seemed exceptionally uncomfortable with the single members of the congregation, as if they were incomplete members, according to family status. While elder teams annually visited the congregational members in their homes for "family visiting," single members were summoned to the church to meet in thirty-minute shifts with the preacher and an elder in the council room—as if the single people didn't have homes.

To me, back then, the preacher seemed uninterested in being a pastor.

Some months after he delivered his Family of God series, I spent three days in the hospital following throat surgery. The first day, the preacher came dutifully to the hospital, read Scripture for fifteen minutes, and prayed so loudly that a passing nurse closed my door. When finally he left the room, the woman in the next bed asked meekly, "Is he your minister?"

"Yeah," I murmured, "he's our preacher."

"Well," she said, "he's sure loud."

God may well have loomed large in his mind and heart, but I'm not sure I did. For that matter, I'm not sure there was room. I know there was none for the woman in the other bed. As a result, there was no room in her heart for him either.

He was, by our perception and estimation, a professional preacher—he proclaimed the Word—loudly. Always, he had an answer, always a scriptural reference, all of it in a voice that seemed dedicated solely to preaching. His sermon points came stepping out of the text; one could outline those sermons every Sunday—and I did. The main points almost aligned themselves, points of admonition and guidelines for living.

He preached quite eloquently, but he didn't really minister to us, or at least to me. We never called him anything but Reverend, nor would he have wanted anything that hinted of familiarity. I suspect that, in spite of his eloquence and diligence, he was quite lonely among us. He was, after all, "the preacher."

We don't use the term preacher so freely these days. Preaching implies, among other things, eloquence in the act of expounding. Today, we might "call a preacher" to serve a church; but once he or she arrives and settles in, we say "Pastor Tom" or "Pastor Mary." Maybe in the past we put too much distance between preaching and ministering—or they did. In my own experience in a number of churches throughout my lifetime, it seems that a good pastor needs either to preach well or minister well; the pastor who can do both is indeed a blessing.

In the early years of my life, I attended a tiny rural church at the edge of the classis, a "little brown church in the dale." We were served, over the years, by some of the most compassionate pastors in the denomination, men (back then) at the beginning or at the end of a preaching career, preachers with seemingly modest aspirations. Serving a little rural church means a pastor must exercise the full range of ministry gifts but on a small scale—certainly, it took humility to go there to the edge of things and probably more humility to stay.

We jokingly claimed to be the extension class of the seminary—seminarians could spend a summer in our midst and try out their "wheat and tares" or "pearls before swine" illustrations in the rural heartland. They'd have a chance to touch a cow or ride a combine or roast hot dogs on a stick over an open fire, but they also had to "serve up the Word" twice a Sunday. I was young, though, and life itself, back then, during my childhood, may seem to me to be simpler than it was.

Back then, every family had a crisis it seemed—a farm foreclosure, a family feud, a prison sentence, an early pregnancy, a terminal illness. One of those preachers, a man I'll call Pastor Ron, served his first charge in our little church and found himself trying to lift the members of that little church up through the most troubling era of their existence. How could one inexperienced pastor minister to all these hurting people?

By God's grace, Pastor Ron did. He listened, he consoled, he prayed, he walked among the hurting. Honestly, next to the preacherly pastor whose sermons were tightly composed, Pastor Ron lit no fires in the pulpit; but his compassion warmed many hearts and often at times when the ability to bring the gospel of love was absolutely essential.

Twenty years later, after the pastor had been serving another congregation, an elderly member of the congregation quipped, "Pastor Ron is coming here next weekend. You know, he never was much of a preacher, but we sure loved him!"

Today, Pastor Ron can preach too.

Good preaching is vital. Churches that go through years of bad preaching suffer death throes. In small communities, the charter members may remain intensely loyal to the body, but when, week after week, preaching comes up short, the church starves.

Today it seems that even the word *preach* has negative connotations. In fact, I advise my writing students not to preach, not to moralize in an obtrusive, pushy manner. Write with vigor, yes, but don't preach. Write the concrete details of a particular experience. Tell the stories, rooted in time and space, stories that grip you, that pain you, that identify the conflict of brokenness and the need for healing, for grace, but don't "preach." At all costs, don't preach.

I wonder, sometimes, how Paul went on preaching with so much conviction that New Testament Jews would kill to have him silenced. Were the messages so new that people could listen for hours without getting restless? What was Paul's preaching mode? Did he study the manuscripts and select a text? Did he preach through a scroll of Isaiah? Did he develop three-point sermons? Did he pray the Psalms?

Of course, in the very early church, the message was new for the converts. Paul and Peter connected the stories of Israelites to the birth and ministry of Jesus. I wonder, though, what kept the older believers coming back to listen. Peter says in his second letter, to those in the faith, "I will always remind you of these things, even though you know them and are firmly established in the truth you now have" (2 Peter 1:12). Sometimes I wonder whether, even in the fledgling church of the apostles, did the excitement wear off?

That's my question every time I hear a boring sermon, which is seldom the case today because my pastor preaches grace-filled sermons that sometimes startle me with the profundity of God's love. He directs us, always, to Scripture, interpreting Scripture with Scripture. He offers no checklists of grace. He works very often with stories. He shows again and again how God used scoundrels—individuals who lied and killed and cheated—to build his church. He calls it "serving up the Word"—not boxed lunches, not fast food, not smorgasbord. He gives us plenty to "chew on," as he says, but there's one enduring theme—the abundant and eternal grace of God.

My pastor uses slightly unconventional words, and sometimes he can't resist an inside joke, but always, he opens up the Word, offering a message with a single point. He doesn't provide sermon outlines, though some very effective preachers do, and he never provides "fill in the blank" check tests to see if we're listening. We usually *are* listening because he makes the familiar texts new.

Good preaching makes good Sundays, but the pastor needs both passion for the Word and compassion for the people in the pew—and the people need passion and compassion too. I wonder sometimes how many pastors suffer a malevolent loneliness in their ministry.

Pastor Tim moved to a small once-thriving church in an academic community, where a stream of students moved in and out of this body of believers. A year earlier, the former pastor had confessed a secret nagging addiction to alcohol and had left the church in division and chaos. The new pastor brought compassion and hope for unity, but the long-time members were tired. It was a small church, and they had carried a heavy load—teaching Sunday School, serving on council, planning worship services, playing the organ, hosting church dinners, cleaning the building, repairing the doors.

A few months after Pastor Tim's arrival, he announced in church that his wife was celebrating a one-year anniversary of being cancer-free. We had no idea that was true.

"That's terrific!" we said to her after the service, and then we simply went on our way.

Later I learned what loneliness Pastor Tim and his wife Linda had suffered from our incidental response to the anniversary of their great joy. They had gone through the valley of near death, and now they asked us to rejoice with them. We didn't know how. We simply didn't know how to share their joy. Nobody gave them flowers—or even a hug. The people who had walked through that valley with Tim and Linda were far away. That entire trauma that we'd not experienced didn't seem to be ours, and we left, smiling. That's all, just smiling.

Their own experience gave them sensitivity and authenticity in ministering to a broken church in what became its dying years—and to hospital patients. One Sunday morning Pastor Tim asked who would be willing to accompany him after the evening service to celebrate the Lord's Supper with a young woman, Brenda, a neo-natal nurse, awaiting a bone marrow transplant in the university hospital. I had known Brenda's mother, so I offered to go, along with another member of the church. Linda, the pastor's wife, didn't go—she couldn't make herself enter another cancer ward.

Thus, on a chilly autumn night, three of us made our way over to the university hospital, Pastor Tim carrying the chalice of wine and part of a loaf of bread. In the bone-marrow ward, we donned white gowns, paper shoe covers, and white paper caps. Then we stepped into Brenda's glass cubicle, where her mother had set up a small keyboard. Clustered around Brenda's bed, a microcosm of the body called "the church," we shared the loaf and sang:

> You satisfy the hungry heart
> with gift of finest wheat.
> Come, give to us, O saving Lord,
> the bread of life to eat.

Brenda lay between us, her red kerchief bright as blood over her smooth white head.

Pastor Tim poured the wine.

> Is not the cup we bless and share
> the blood of Christ out-poured?
> Do not one cup, one loaf, declare
> our oneness in the Lord?

We sang with hope. The bone marrow would be implanted on Tuesday. Brenda's body seemed ready to accept new life.

> You give yourself to us, O Lord;
> then selfless let us be
> to serve each other in your name
> in truth and charity.

Body life—right then and there, we were members implanted with the blood of Christ.

The church, meanwhile, struggled on. Pastor Tim supported a developing Friendship Ministry for people with disabilities, he "served up the Word" with plenty to chew on, and he encouraged the growth of stimulating Bible studies. The body should have grown stronger, but it didn't. Instead, it seemed to totter and grow progressively weaker.

In April, we went one more time to Brenda's ward to celebrate communion. Pastor Tim carried the chalice and the loaf—the portion left from that Sunday's morning service, one loaf of many grains.

This time we didn't need the paper gear. We didn't go behind glass. We clustered around the bed. Pastor Tim placed a hand of blessing on Brenda's head, and again we sang:

> You satisfy the hungry heart
> with gifts of finest wheat . . .
> Come, give to us, O saving Lord,
> the bread of life to eat.

Pastor Tim opened the Word, broke the loaf, poured the wine. Once more we sang:

> . . . then selfless let us be
> to serve each other in your name
> in truth and charity.

Three days later, we learned that Brenda was dying. The transplant had failed. Pastor Tim told me on Wednesday night at church, after Friendship class. "Go and say good-bye," he urged me. Brenda was leaving the hospital and going home to die.

I drove across town to the hospital, wondering what language is right for dying. I had no appropriate words, and so, for several minutes I simply hugged her, this daughter of my own high school friend. "I'm sorry," I said quietly.

"It's okay," she said. "I'm going home tomorrow. Maybe I have a few months yet."

"I'll never forget," I told her, "that we shared the body and blood of Christ, here in this room. And now, after all these months, you're leaving—but Christ has prepared a place for you."

"Yes," she said. "I don't have to live in isolation anymore."

I will never forget the pastor's sending me to speak to her that final time, but a few months later Brenda died.

Sadly enough, so did the church. Within a couple of years, Pastor Tim had accepted another call, and eventually the little church was gone. Who can explain the demise of a church that once thrived? Maybe its time had come.

The church in that city may well be gone, but I carry lifelong memories of its ministry—of unforgettable moments when the preacher was a pastor who ministered to the lives of the saints, when he helped me be a pastor too, in a way I will not forget.

In my years in various churches, I have been asked to participate in its ministries—I have been included in its mission and task. During those years, I have also been excluded, treated as if I were not a vital part of the congregation.

For all of us, pastors and parishioners alike, perseverance—not attaining longevity or building successful programs or practicing preacherliness—is the measure of faithful ministry, serving up the Word.

For Further Reflection

The pastor Van Gilst identifies as "the preacher" rather clearly failed to communicate with her—and others. Yet, it seems by her description that he thought himself firmly grounded in the Word. How is that possible? How can pastors, committed to the Word, guard against becoming so narrow in their applications of the gospel to which they are deeply devoted that they miss the important realities in the lives of their parishioners? Is that a problem of character or a problem of theology?

Here, as elsewhere in the stories these writers tell, small moments of intimacy seem most memorable when the writers recount their experiences of strong and effective pastoral work. Can pastors create programs that offer opportunities for such intimacy, or do they simply develop on their own, serendipitously, by God's own council?

"Perseverance," she says, "is the measure of faithful ministry." How do we learn perseverance? Is Job the only biblical example, or are there others? What pastors do you know who have it? Is it a gift of age and experience?

CHAPTER 7

Lost in the Pew

Jack VandenBorn

At the heart of all religious experience, ironically—and biblically—is the loss of self. Simply stated, we come near unto God only when we shed much of who and what we are. Pentecostals delight in such moments, when, emptied of self, they are "filled with the Holy Spirit." One does not need to be charismatic, however, to know that spiritual experience occurs only in moments like those Jack VandenBorn describes as being "lost." In this biographical essay, he walks us through sixty years of church attendance and urges pastors to help their congregations get lost in the joy of Christ.

> O, Jesus joy of loving hearts, the fount of life, the light of men
> From fullest bliss that earth imparts, we turn unfilled to you again.
> We turn unfilled to you again.
>
> Psalter Hymnal #307

Lost, Version One

On a fresh Saturday morning in mid-April 2004, two friends and I headed southeast from Houston, British Columbia, into the backcountry and arrived at our site by 9:00 a.m.—Equity Mine Road's kilometre 33. The day was sweet, on the edge of freezing, bright sunshine, the snow a delight, glistening and glinting with what the three of us read as the sparkle of the Lord.

The snow had melted and frozen in the last weeks again and again, so that the three or four-foot snow pack had a four- or five-inch crust, a crust that easily kept us on top. Gorgeous, go-wherever-you-like skiing, the gliding slick and fast—"the fullest bliss earth imparts."

My dog Max was with us, happy to run and sniff along the ski path with ease, no falling through the crust for him either.

We had skied the path a dozen times in the past decade, a doughnut trail centered and surrounded by pine and spruce. Our trail was clear and wide, a treeless swamp that swept northwest for a couple of kilometres, turned clockwise on a radius of five hundred metres, and swung back southeast to the road, an easy five or six kilometer run, a nearly divine Saturday morning.

Can church services be like that? Gorgeous, pristine, profoundly satisfying, like the fullest bliss earth imparts, sweeping one away into a reverie? into an enchantment? Like a great story?

Sometimes a book or movie takes us over, and, we say, "I got lost in the story." The reading or viewing experience gathers intensity and overpowers our normal self-awareness. We lose our self; it's ravishing.

Lost, Version Two

It's also possible to get lost so that a person doesn't know where he or she is. That can be fearful.

So it was that on that April morning two of us decided to add a short detour, a kilometer along the power line to the edge of a ravine. On the return, we decided to cut through the bush to meet our partner at the corner of the turn by 9:30. We couldn't miss the way.

The time for our rendezvous passed, as did noon … as did two o'clock.

We saw only trees, and trees, and trees. We kept telling ourselves that we had only to head southeast to get to the road, but the road did not appear—until 7:00 p.m.

By ten that morning, Jean, the third of our threesome, the one who had not departed from the route as we had, was deeply worried, frantic by noon. She stopped a passing vehicle and asked the driver to alert the RCMP. She couldn't understand how her two companions could get lost. We had skied the trail a dozen times. Had one of us broken a limb? Had we tried going down the ravine? Had one had a heart attack? Could a bear have attacked?

Rescuers began arriving around two. The police vehicle wailed its siren regularly—we heard it. Not much later, the clatter of a helicopter punctured the silence. Search and rescue volunteers tried their snowmobiles, but the snow could not hold them. The evergreen canopy kept us hidden until seven that night when we finally emerged onto Equity Mine Road, into the presence of the rescuers.

Pew Sitting Sixty Years

I've been a pew sitter in the Christian Reformed Church of North America for more than sixty years. In that time, I've probably attended more than forty-five hundred services, maybe five thousand.

I grew up in Alberta in the 1950s and attended two church services every Sunday—at 10:00 am and 1:30 p.m.; the short time between services intended to make it easier for the out-of-town families to stay in town.

For a time, we country folk had lunch with the same town-dwelling family every Sunday. Later, we ate our lunch in church.

After lunch, a couple of other kids and I could walk around town. When I was fifteen, I was allowed to drive our truck around town—even though I was without a driver's license. Small town life, back then, was not fussy.

One Sunday, while I was driving around a rain-slicked racetrack at the fair grounds, the truck slipped off the track and ran into a tree—$300 damage to the grill. No more trucking between services and no driver's license for several years.

The church we attended consisted mainly of newly immigrated families from the Netherlands. Dutch was its natural language. Within a year or two, the youngsters acquired English at school, and we snickered and later howled about the mangled English from the pulpit: "time-o-thy" for "Timothy," "poom" for "poem," "dirty-too" for "thirty-two." A few years later, my father, perpetually an elder, became very upset with mispronunciations emanating from our immigrant preacher. "I don't understand why he doesn't take speaking lessons," he said.

When it was time to do professions of faith, Dad amusingly replayed the questioning he had done about movie attendance at the meeting the previous evening. It seemed all the young people went to movies, but he never voted against accepting any of them for full church membership, even though to him, movies, like card playing and dancing, were "from the devil."

Two of my older brothers and I smiled, not believing. We were becoming Canadians.

No, we were already Canadians.

****

"Assimilation" is the technical phrasing for what was my life experience in those days. I wanted badly to be a Canadian, to be seen as just one more Canadian kid at school. The Dutchisms of church, as well as the church's odd restrictions (*odd* when my classmates talked about necking at drive-in movies and dancing on weekends) were embarrassments for me in high school where I didn't talk at all about our little church on the highway close to the edge of town.

As the 1960s began, my assimilation process continued, more dramatically, in Edmonton, at the big university.

My education didn't start well. My dad dropped me off to register for courses and went on to do his egg business. I was supposed to call him at my sister's house late in the afternoon, but I had never used a telephone with a dial. "Lift the receiver. Listen for a dial tone. Dial the desired number."

I lifted the receiver, heard the dial tone, put the receiver down and dialed. After completing the dialing, I lifted the receiver and heard what I couldn't identify as a busy signal. Again, and again, and again.

In the fall of 1960, as I was assimilating into university life, I had to determine what my church life would be. There were no older brothers to smooth the way, no cousins to help find a friendly church building, no chaplains to soothe a questioning teenager. Getting lost in the crowd of university roommates became the option, the ready-to-hand choice. We went to class; to labs; learned what was in the library; studied for hours; and figured out how to catch a movie downtown, play cards, order "Chicken-on-the-Way," and slug a beer.

I don't recall exactly how I found the First Christian Reformed Church on the other side of the North Saskatchewan River. I knew about the church and had been there a number of times; my sister and several older brothers were, or had been, members. None of them, though, lived in my new university world.

It was probably the Edmonton Transit System that showed the way to worship in that first year of university life away from home, although not every Sunday, and certainly not twice.

The next summer I returned home to the farm and full churchly regularity.

During the next academic year, I met a young woman at a church-organized bowling night, a wondrous girl whose first burning kiss began a romance now more than forty years old. She worked at a bank and held my hand at the places we went to. Avlyn's parents had been members of the First CRC fifteen years earlier; the two of us easily and naturally became a couple in that church.

With this "joining together," the assimilation process formed me into a Canadian-Christian more gracefully. We married in 1964, and, within a few years, I was taken into the church's inner circles as a full-fledged defender of the faith, a proponent—no longer the explorer earlier at the university.

Attending church services, pew sitting, became a habit we chose as part of our lifestyle. Avlyn sang in a choir, and I went to a season of Men's Society meetings.

As I recall, though, a certain kind of emptiness permeated the services back then, as if the Christianity I was in and practicing concerned a world I didn't really inhabit at all. Its conceptual content, its language, and its rituals seemed somehow foreign to the world I lived in daily. Not offensive, not bothersome, no longer embarrassing—yet not essentially compelling, not a life calling. My recollection now is that I must have thought that participating in church life was like brushing your teeth—healthy, positive, and just plain good for you.

I suppose I didn't understand the Christian life as having much to do with the social, political, and cultural elements of Edmonton, Alberta, and the 1960s. I didn't even know that a social, political, or cultural world existed. I mean I knew that political, social, and cultural events took place, but to add them up into a "world" and to think that an alternative world was somehow possible did not enter into my thought processes at the time.

To be sure, Avlyn and I sometimes attended meetings set up by the Christian Action Foundation, the Calvin Club, the Association of Reformed Scientific Studies, and perhaps others I don't recall. Gradually, we learned, vaguely, that creating an alternate cultural world was the specific intent of those groups. These Christians, predominately Dutch immigrants, aimed to produce a "kingdom of God" in Edmonton, in Canada, a vast cultural transformation.

During the second half of the decade of the 1960s, while much of North America brewed with cultural change—long hair, bell-bottom jeans, the Beatles, illegal drugs, university sit-ins, unseating a government—I sat comfortably in church every Sunday, warmly embraced by a family of two children, a new house, a secure job teaching school, maybe Saturday night hockey.

No envisioning cultural transformation. Not yet.

Curiously, in the years 1970-1974, my seat on the pew, five rows up from the back on the left, took on a new orientation. A new magic entered into my understanding. A new preacher had entered our life, and quickly Christianity, in my mind, became a muscled giant playing in the arena of cultural design. The preacher's sermons were stunningly spirited, resonating shapers of deep understanding. We loved those church services and sermons, got carried away by them like skiing in spring sunlight. Lost in the pew, lost in a heavenly delight. Maybe the "fullest bliss that earth imparts." Maybe the "fullest bliss that earth imparts."

"We turned—filled by you again."

More than thirty years later, I still feel as if I can lay out the line of thought of various sermons: a series on Jonah, "Blessed Are the Peacemakers," Christian schooling at our son's baptism service. Our family didn't skip church services in those days in order to have a picnic on a forest cut block or to go to the lake.

Those four years transformed our hearts—powerful Kuyperian notes banged inside the walls of our minds. Within a few years, I was back in school, graduate school in Calvin College. Those Kuyperian notes needed clarification, development, and force. I wanted to learn better where and how Christians could contribute to, improve, and transform their cultural circumstances.

2006

Today, my wife and I, now grandparents, feel that we are "free agents" with respect to church membership. Even though we have been members of the Christian Reformed Church for all of our lives, we're quite able to switch. We don't believe the CRC somehow holds the only keys to the eternal kingdom. If the style of worship, the kind of singing, the texture of the preaching, the overall direction of a church's own sense of mission doesn't suit us, in time we'll find a church more favourable to our disposition.

More than a thousand miles away in Michigan, my brother-in-law and his wife feel the same way—he more than she. Wearied by years of intense participation in Sunday school teaching, church council meetings, Bible study groups, cadets, and choir, they now attend a mega-church where they hear great music and great sermons and are free of possessive, confining, implacable demands for involvement. It's *distance* he wants, a steel fence around churchly obligations.

In an earlier era for them, and for us, say, the 1950s-1980s, church obligations seemingly superseded all other obligations and possibilities. Our two families, both CRC but a country apart, felt a similar kind of commitment to our fellowships; I suppose many church councils even expected that kind of solid commitment.

Some things haven't changed. Last spring, I was asked to let my name stand for the position of elder—which was all right. If I thought I couldn't take on the task, I was told that I would have to come to a meeting of the church council to explain why.

Hoop-de-do, I thought. We live in Canada, not Calvin's Geneva, not today's China. That kind of coercion simply doesn't exist in Western civilization. We are not some kind of vassal to a churchly liege. Today it seems to me we owe the church only that which we may care to offer.

Last summer, we attended my brother-in-law's mega-church. After the welcome, we stood up to sing three, maybe four songs. A family was interviewed briefly about their one-week mission trip to the Ukraine. The collection and a special song followed. Then the Bible reading, an orderly sermon, and a closing prayer—and we were finished. Less than an hour. Wow. Felt great.

My brother-in-law makes his financial donations in cash—can't be tracked or traced. I suppose he prefers to keep his financial account with God, not the church board.

In an article titled "Dieting for Jesus," in *Prospect Magazine*, Alan Wolfe, professor at Boston College, explains that our two families aren't unique in North America:

> Denominational affiliations mean little in the US. American culture is highly individualistic, and resists strong organizational ties. Labor unions, political parties, sports franchises and business corporations have all been hollowed out as Americans have come to think of themselves as free agents who sell their talents and interests to the highest bidders . . . a third to a half of America's believers have changed denominations in the course of their lives.

What I feel today—what my brother and I and our wives now feel—isn't particularly extraordinary, I suppose.

Church Services

I once watched a documentary about the preparations for a rock concert, a U2 concert, I think, an event scheduled for the Fleetwood Center in Boston. Ten semitrailer loads of equipment were involved: staging, loudspeakers, mixing boards, monitor speakers, lights, giant video screens. Large numbers of people—laborers and technical experts—unloaded, then hauled, set up, arranged, tested the equipment, rearranged, and tested again, so that the impact on eighty thousand fans would be staggering.

Two of our church members attended a U2 concert in Vancouver last year. The concert astonished them, they said, laddered them to a musical high they could not have imagined.

Couldn't church services be like that? At least a little?

While church services are not rock concerts, worship planners would do well to absorb whatever wisdom rock concerts, concert halls, movie theaters, and sports arenas can offer. Today, people attend church worship, in part—and in larger and larger part—because of the attracting force of the events themselves, their magnetism, their spectacle—and less and less, as I once did, from a musty memory of duty.

Mega-churches work because they have adopted that lesson. They have created spectacular auditoriums, buildings, and landscaping, a dazzling stage area, gleaming sound, and snappy sermons. Churches become mega-churches because today people *choose* to attend them because they *want* to attend them, not because they think, somehow, that they are obligated to attend, that attendance at worship is part of their cultural task.

Assembling a fetching worship service is hardly an easy task—it's not just to sing together a salad from the gray hymnal, the overhead song box, a prayer or two, a sermon, a benediction, and "it's a wrap."

The strategies and planning should aim to make it easy for parishioners to get "lost in the pew," *lost* in the sense of being carried away by the "story."

The power of the service should bring listeners into the flow of the service's elements so that their inner sense of time vanishes. The elements need to glide from one to the other effortlessly, the transitions all shadowing themselves into the background. The experience of the service could feel like a book or movie that overtakes one's sense of self and pastes it into the sweep of the grand gospel narrative.

As with any formal event, the audience needs to be welcomed, heartily. A brief Bible passage and an opening song foreshadow a celebratory hour. My wife and I love singing—old hymns, sacred music, some praise songs. Music is simply a great joy for us in all kinds of settings. We begin Sunday mornings at home with a CD of choral music. Choirs attract our voices from time to time. If I lead a church service when the pastor is gone, an extra hymn or two easily sneaks into the order of service.

In making the church service flow gracefully and grippingly, it seems to me the worship leader could take on more of the role of a kind of conductor, more that, and less a master of ceremonies. A master of ceremonies aims to make sure everyone knows what to do by carefully announcing a song number, perhaps saying it twice—in case someone didn't catch it. In our congregation, the numbers are listed in a bulletin and on a number board at the front of the church. The kind of conductor I envision is one who assumes that more or less everyone knows what to do and needs only to signal the way forward with minor indicators, as a symphony orchestra conductor does, permitting the audience to lose themselves in the unfolding elements that constitute worship. To that end, all worship leaders need to avoid drawing attention to themselves and recognize that their directing of events can as easily be interruptive as it can be helpful.

The Sermon

The sermon became central to worship in the Reformational avalanche of the 1500s. I'm not sure what sermons were like in the thousand years prior to that time, but my sense is that the most significant liturgical change created by the Reformation was that sermons became long—too long, far too long.

In the May 2005 issue of a *Focus on the Family* publication, Kurt Bruner writes, "I grew up attending churches that used expository teaching. Each Sunday the pastor would invite the congregation to 'open your Bibles' to the passage for his sermon. Then we would expect the next 30 to 40 minutes to include three points, a poem and two application lessons, while we wondered, *When will this end?*" Bruner recommends that story formats replace the three-point, expository sermon: "The themes of the gospel are often better depicted than described." Make it a story, he says, with emotional content, with characters in conflict, or in grace.

Maybe.

During many a sermon, I easily get lost in the pew in the way I got lost skiing in the bush, lost and completely out of touch. All I hear is words, words, words, just as all I saw in the bush were trees, trees, trees.

My father once described a sermon, perhaps someone's sermonizing, as an activity like "splashing around in a swimming pool," lots of banging on the water, lots of short spurts, lots of standing on the bottom—an intense vocal ramble, a staccato peppering of paragraphs, a barrage of thought.

"It's been thirty years of boring sermons in my church," said one man to my brother. Thirty years of ramble and splatter, I suppose.

My sense is that many sermons have individual paragraphs that hold together, but lack the snug coherence that makes for easy listening. As an English teacher, it strikes me that achieving coherence in extended writing or speaking is exceptionally difficult. Our normal mental operations, I think, are a motley splatter of images, ideas, and memory. Arraying or wedging them into some manner of sensibility requires a thread along which coherence can develop, a healthy organizing thread plus a lot of cutting and arranging. Not at all an easy task.

Ordinary conversation, however, is full of ramble and splatter, yet it seldom feels incoherent. Conversations flow effortlessly, jump around from topic to topic, and nearly always register as sane by the participants. Strange.

I'd guess, though, that the topics of conversation generally remain brief—two minutes, five minutes, certainly less than ten. Maybe it's the conciseness that makes understanding and coherence easy.

Many sermons, or so it seems to me, tend to ramble and splatter. I don't particularly fault preachers for sermons weak in coherence, but I thank the Lord for the occasional sermon of power, sermons that bless us deeply. Like first-rate stories that stay in our memory easily, these sermons remain readily available to our thoughts, some after as many as thirty years later for me. The line of coherence remains, and one's memory can reconstruct the details.

The sermons that get through to me usually have these characteristics:

- They lean away from simplistically telling listeners what to do—for example, to pray more, to be more loyal, to love more, to make faith ever stronger, to grow spiritually.
- They provide spiritually mature folks with a critique of the biblical text—a considered judgment of, or a discussion about the character or qualities of the text under consideration.
- They try to relate the text to the current culture.
- They fill in the key events of stories with rich detail.
- They keep it short.

Last Words

Cynthia Ozick, in explaining her favourite kind of writing (novels over essays), in *Heir to a Glimmering World* (2004) notes,

> ...when a novel's sinews are bound up in the most fearful intimations of language, when setting down a phrase feels tantamount to ingesting the blood of demon[s] . . . just *there* is the difference between the safety of prose and the lust of art: think of the haying scene in *Anna Karenina*, or the Marabar caves in *A Passage to India*. Call it language, call it intuition, call it seduction, call it idea-as-emotion. It is a voluptuousness only the novel knows, an elusive grail we poor scribblers helplessly chase.

Those few superior and memorable sermons I recall contain something of that kind of voluptuousness. They spilled a seduction of some mix of gripping parable and pressing insight into our ears. The words somehow unearthed a splendid cogency from a biblical passage. Those sermons remain for years, maybe longer.

In a November 2005 article in the *London Telegraph*, Elizabeth Day quotes one preacher who remembered being taught that "for every minute preached, an hour must be spent in preparation. The aim of a good sermon," he said, "is to give a message in an illuminating and entertaining way. For a vicar," Ms. Day continues, "a perfect sermon would stirringly convey the profundity of religious truth and the beauty of God's work in each and every one of us." Then, she adds, "for a congregation, a perfect sermon would be, well, short."

"I'm extremely brief," Father Michael Seed, from Westminster Cathedral, told Day. "My sermons are not more than five minutes long, partly because I don't make notes. If you can't say something in five minutes, you might as well give up. A bishop friend of mine says that when I'm preaching, the congregation 'hangs off' every word because there are so few of them."

When a sermon uncovers or unveils something of the Lord's power, I get wonderfully lost—not lost in some woods where every tree painfully obscures the horizon, but, instead, I lose myself in the brilliance of unfolding disclosures and poetic understanding. My self-awareness dissipates, and I am taken down a roadway of clarity by the sermon's progress, a journey of understanding from opening to dazzling opening into the miracle of grace. Something like that.

Coherent, pointed, concise. A voluptuous opening out of the darkened bush, a place to get lost in the glory of the gospel's promise, lost in this world, His world. Help us get there. Help us home.

As the old song says, help us, each week, in all of our unfilledness "to turn to Him again."

For Further Reflection

In the process of telling us his story, VandenBorn puts his finger on a dramatic truth about the contemporary church: Denominations, today, simply don't matter as much as they once did. Choice is all. "Today, people attend church worship, in part—and in larger and larger part—because of the attracting force of the events themselves," he writes, "their magnetism, their spectacle—and less and less, as I once did, from a musty memory of duty."

Do you agree? If he's right—and he certainly is right about himself—then how does his analysis alter the way in which we do church or think of church? What are the advantages of this new vision or things—church as option and not requirement? What are the disadvantages?

Two growing fellowships in North America, oddly enough and despite their incredible differences, are the Pentecostals and the Orthodox. Both generally have very long weekly worship services. VandenBorn insists that sermons be short? Do you agree or disagree?

CHAPTER 8

What is Ours and What is His—Knowing the Difference

Matthew Ackerman

Among the seemingly myriad roles pastors have to carry out is football coach—not literally, of course; all pastors, at some point in their professional lives, have to be motivational speakers because motivation is something required of any leader. Matt Ackerman, the youngest of the essayists, a recent Calvin College graduate, reflects on the ways good pastors have motivated him in his life. In so doing, he tells stories that offer the rest of us models for successful ministries—even, and maybe even especially, to young people.

The thought of being a pastor scares me. It always has. The job is a combination of difficult tasks, most of which make me queasy all by themselves. Imagining them together is enough to make anyone feel completely overwhelmed. Yet, as hard as the job can be, it seems to me that some pastors I've known have appeared determined to make the job even harder on themselves.

Thankfully, God does not ask pastors to do it all, nor should we, their congregations, ask them to. The temptation to control everything is very strong, I'm sure, as is the temptation for us—members of congregations—to want them to do just that. To combat those desires while equipping their flocks for service, pastors must be humble, trusting, and passionate. I am quite sure that, in the years the Lord gives me in my life, I'll learn more and more and more about how pastors operate, how they deal with the pressures that come at them from all sides. I'd like to offer some stories from the life of a twenty-something. What follows are four stories that I've not forgotten, stories that define at least something of what it means to me—at least at this point in my life—to be a successful pastor, one who shares the burdens, who leads with grace and a smile.

The Truth in Love

I will never forget the Sunday my mom passed on the communion plate without stopping to take a piece of Christ's body, broken for us. I was 11 years old, and I had seen her take communion four times a year for as long as I could remember. I even used to pop a peppermint in my mouth just as the pastor would say, "Take, eat, remember, and believe," so I could pretend I was doing it too.

This particular Sunday, though, I knew something was decidedly wrong. Her posture seemed cramped, her face tight, her hands clenched in a death grip, her lips pulled pencil-thin—and I knew that look. It was the same one she gave me when I harassed my older sisters beyond a reasonable limit. It meant trouble, and not just a little bit.

I had never seen her take on that look in church before. Even when my sisters and I whispered or drew silly pictures on the bulletin, we just got the pinch (a terrible fate in its own right). The look she wore that day she normally deemed too private for Sunday morning worship. What I saw was unprecedented and surprising. I was mostly glad it wasn't because of something I had done.

At that time, I had just learned that being "a mason" could mean more than knowing how to cut stone. I knew there had been some discussions of this mysterious group recently, mostly because my bedroom was well placed to eavesdrop on my parents' late-night discussions when my father returned from meetings with the other elders.

Our church had several founding members, including one elder, who were Freemasons—that much I knew. They were the type of people who form the backbone of any church, dedicated servants who take Christ's call on their lives seriously and place great emphasis on loyalty. As my father put it, "For them, being a Mason is kind of like being part of the Boy Scouts. If the Masons had made them choose between their church and being a Mason, they would have stayed with the church."

The denomination of which we were a part of at that time had made no definitive statement on whether lodge membership was a good or bad thing, but the pastor had initiated a discussion of the issue within the council, as I learned years later. His firm stance was that a person's committing to a society like the Masons was inconsistent with the membership vows these men had made to the church. He had proposed a private ultimatum, of sorts, that made it clear these families had to choose between membership in the Masons and membership in that congregation. The other elders were not so sure. Even those who agreed with the pastor in principle (the majority of the council, including my own father) were undecided about how the issue should be handled.

That was how things had been left, or so I'm told, when that fateful Sunday arrived. The council had decided that something needed to be done to address this—memberships in both organizations was not acceptable—but they had not yet determined the nature of that decision. The families who maintained memberships in the Masons had been members of the church for decades; without them that congregation might not have survived some of its more difficult times.

As part of his sermon that Sunday, the pastor spoke out forcefully and even reproachfully about membership in the Masons. He was unequivocal in his stance, and the shock waves that rippled through the sanctuary were powerful enough for even an 11 year old to remember vividly.

The fallout was predictable: Many of those families never set foot in that church again, most of the elders were upset with the pastor, while some members saw no problem with the way things had transpired.

For me, what remains is the memory of my mother's face that morning. Never before had I seen her look that way in church, or had I known her to refuse to partake of the sacrament. She later explained that she had felt far too angry and bitter to do so.

Amazingly, my mother was someone who agreed with what our pastor had said.

Pastors are called to speak prophetically to their congregations, and part of that task means being able to identify sin in the life of the church and its members. In defense of this pastor, he never changed his stance or was ambiguous in his condemnation of Masonic membership. From his first day in that church, he made his views clear, and has since been supported by the denomination of which he is a part.

The problem for my mother, however, was the manner, the tone, by which he addressed the problem. He communicated a sense that he was the only one doing the work of the church. He did not display—at least at the moment—the humility and love that should accompany any prophetic word from a pastor.

Leading Without Crashing

It takes courage to start something, but it takes even more to let some things fail. Imagine you are a pastor working on a vibrantly Christian campus. Many traditional outlets exist for students to explore, express, and expand their faith; but something appears to be missing. Along with a small group of students, you recognize a need for nontraditional approaches to faith, and you seek a way to address that need.

On one such campus, a small but dedicated group spent several years building up an alternative worship service under the leadership of an ordained campus minister. This unique and creative event attracted a faithful following among the student body and was praised as a cutting-edge experiment in postmodern worship. Each week it consisted of prayers, poems, Scripture readings, and live jazz music all focusing on a broad topic.

In its first years, this experiment went through its share of growing pains. Some of the original goals of the service—such as reaching out to members of the community jazz scene and providing a way for students to get beyond the bubble of the college by meeting off campus—were not met. However, the worship experience was a success and continued for over three years, first as a college-sponsored event and after as a student-run club.

For some of us who were involved with the project, the role that our pastor took often seemed confusing, even maddening. He was as committed and passionate about the idea as we were, but things that seemed like disasters to us never appeared to bother him. A semester into the first full year, the student leader, along with her boyfriend, decided to study abroad, leaving the team down two key members and without clear choices for replacements. In this worrisome time, our intrepid leader assured us that the ministry was God's, not ours. If this was the end of the experiment, so be it. If not, God would provide—as he did.

At times, this distancing felt to some of us like a betrayal. We wondered how he could step away like that. Didn't he care what happened?

As I got to know him better, I realized that he cared a great deal about what happened, but his personal investment in the program did not define him. His devotion to that work ran deep, yet he was able to keep enough distance to maintain perspective and eventually turn the whole operation over to others. If this new alternative worship experience had failed miserably, this pastor would not have lost faith in God or himself.

None of us likes to fail, but it seems that the key to failing well is remembering who we are in Christ. Our identity as children of God, chosen by grace through no merit of our own, frees us from worrying about failure. It is to a life of faithfulness that we are called, not to success necessarily. We can approach all our endeavors trusting that God will see us through for his own purposes.

No matter how difficult it is for any of us, it seems that failing is especially difficult for pastors. They need to see their work as far more than simply an occupation, of course, but, paradoxically, they also need to see it simply as a job. A congregation should not underestimate how vitally important their pastor's calling is to equip God's people for service, but neither should the people place the weight of all that work on their shoulders alone.

Our pastors—like all of us—need always to remember that the God who has called them, works through them. The hard work of ministry does not belong to pastors, denominations, congregations, or even the church universal. That hard work is God's and God's alone. We are his tools, his instruments, to be used for his purposes.

I'm sure that finding the balance can be difficult. Pastors especially, it seems, want to invest themselves heavily in their work, perhaps because they must so often deal with the extremely weighty stuff. Great danger is in store for both the pastor and the ministry if an emotional attachment, a determined drive to rid the world of its problems, becomes too strong. When pastors begin to equate the success or failure of the ministry with their success or failure, they have stopped trusting the God we all serve.

The Reformed tradition of "the priesthood of all believers" reminds us that a sense of God's own call is not something given to pastors alone. All of us are called to ministry, no matter what we do. We all must find the right balance of committing ourselves to ministry in all our various walks of life, and, at the same time, creating sufficient distance from immediate and long-term results if for no other reason than that those long-term results belong to God.

Hoop Dreams

All we wanted to do was put up a basketball hoop. We never realized it would be such a problem. The house where I was living with five other students and a mentor was a college-sponsored intentional Christian community in a relatively impoverished neighborhood. Our goal in living there together was twofold: develop strong internal community that would build one another up in faith and develop strong relationships with our neighbors and serve them in whatever way we could. Our partners in this goal were our college and the church that owned our home, their former parsonage. We were able to serve as liaisons of sorts between the church and the neighborhood, especially by helping out with established church programs.

Most of our interaction with the neighborhood was with kids under the age of 14. While it was wonderful for our place to be a sort of community center where neighborhood kids could get help with homework, play games, or simply hang around while we went about our daily lives, we had hoped to get to know a broader spectrum of our community than simply the kids. Teenage boys and young men were around a lot, but we had no medium for engaging them. Teenage boys aren't really into Twister. What they did enjoy was basketball.

Our plan was to put up a basketball hoop in the church parking lot, right in front of the parsonage and the parking spots we used every day. We knew there had been a hoop in an unsupervised area on the far side of the church, but it had been destroyed. It was our hope that we could control use of this hoop with our cars and perhaps a locking mechanism on the rim. We would buy it with house funds and provide the labor for its installation.

We brought our idea to the church's building committee, and they approved it. After we bought the materials, we went to the committee again and asked if they could suggest someone to advise us on how to best install the hoop. Our backs were strong but we lacked expertise and experience. They recommended a gang of retired men from the congregation, many of whom had construction experience, a group who met one weekday morning each week to do odd jobs around the church while enjoying one another's company. These men were, in a way, representative of the whole church: graciously generous with their time and faithful in their commitment to service.

That is why I was stunned when I went to them for help and was met with severe resistance. The morning I was to make my request I found them, along with our pastor, still enjoying their morning coffee before setting out on their day's work. After a few minutes of small talk, I got down to business and asked if they could help us by sharing their knowledge. What I got instead was a litany of reasons why putting a basketball hoop in the church parking lot was a terrible idea, including that it would be destroyed by rough play in a matter of weeks and that the young men from the neighborhood were sure to use the drainage gutter near the church entrance to relieve themselves, gracing the area with an unmistakable odor.

In the middle of the discussion (which wasn't much of a discussion), I looked to our pastor for support; after all he knew of the building committee's decision to support our plan. To my dismay he agreed with the consensus—it was a foolish idea.

When I tried to formulate an explanation as to why we thought the hoop would be helpful in our neighborhood, the men made it clear that they would have no part in the venture, and our pastor looked on in silence. Eventually, however, the hoop went up with the help of one of the members of that group, after which our pastor thanked us—from the pulpit—for donating it.

I was frustrated by the mixed messages we received and hurt by our pastor's unexpected lack of support, even though we had followed the proper channels in our request. To his credit, when I told him I was hurt by his lack of reaction, he apologized.

That's not the end of the story. Within two months, the hoop had been destroyed, and nearly all of the problems I had been warned of manifested themselves, including the odors. Drawing from their years of experience, the men—and our pastor—had predicted exactly what would happen. Our plan to control the hoop's use was naive and maybe even a bit foolish, our youthful exuberance imprudent.

We learned the truth the hard way, by our own experience. The coffee gang predicted what was going to happen, but we didn't believe them.

However, outright prohibition wouldn't have taught us much but antipathy; we would have been angered by their stubbornness. Pastors—and councils and even loosely organized bands of retired gentlemen—need to offer the people of the church, and maybe the young people especially, the opportunities to learn, not simply by precept but also by experience.

Motivation

Calvin College's chaplain, Dale Cooper, has inspired generations of students in his decades at the school, and his reputation for tireless devotion to those students is well deserved. However, he'll be the first to tell you the key is not how much he does, but rather how he does what he does.

One of the first things students discover when they meet "Coop," as his students affectionately call him, is that he lives with passion—his exuberant cheerleading, working a crowd of students one-third his age into a frenzy at basketball games—and a touch of gracious eccentricity—his beloved John Deere tractor parked outside his campus office. Many students discover that when they have good news—whether an engagement, a job, or simply a good grade on a test—no one is happier for them than Coop.

Few people I know are more passionate about the Heidelberg Catechism or Calvin's *Institutes* than he is, and that passion translates especially well to his ministry with young people.

Coop asked directly for only one job in all his years at Calvin College, and he waited until his third decade to do it. As director of the Jubilee Fellows Program, he teaches a seminar course that encourages students to ask tough questions about ministry and calling, then sends those students out to churches and ministries on summer internships. One summer, not long ago, I was one of those sent, full of enthusiasm.

By the time Coop came for his scheduled visit half way into my internship, I was bewildered and discouraged by the confusing things I had encountered. The church where I worked was like nothing I had ever seen. Coop was wonderfully understanding and sympathetic, but what I remember most from that visit, and what got me through that summer was his excitement about the opportunity with which I had been presented. He heard my tales of woe and then encouraged me to approach things with a positive attitude and a more open mind. The irony of a 60-plus-college professor's telling a 21-year-old college student to relax and go with the flow was not lost on me.

His passion was infectious. Before I knew it, I was even using his trademark phrases to express my joy when I ran into new things.

Many of his students throughout the years will say the same thing: The enthusiasm with which he serves others inspires them to service themselves.

****

Motivation is a strange thing. Many times we cannot create it in ourselves, but just one word from someone else will do it for us. A kind expression of gratitude or simply a moment of concentrated recognition can push us to do things we never thought possible. A little joy and passion are sometimes all it takes to get things moving.

Motivation means getting people to buy into a broader vision than the one that ends at their own noses. It seems to me that if you paint a picture of the vast height, width, and depth of the kingdom, people will respond. In situations that require some hard work or difficult negotiations, pastors need to show their congregations exactly what is at stake. Show us the needs of the world, and they are great, and then equip us to meet them.

It is easy to say that pastors do too much, but then, all of us know that there is much to be done because pain and suffering is all around us—pain and suffering the church is called to ease. From the bulletins to the sermons and from the food drive to the service project, the work never seems to end. Yet, no pastor can do it all, or even coordinate it all.

It can be tempting to turn to guilt to motivate, but that is a poor substitute for a genuine spirit of servanthood. Congregations, young people in particular, are more inspired by the dramatic vision of God's plan for his world than they are by a serious and well-meant diet of "shoulds." Pastors should never succumb to scaring people into action.

Becoming a pastor seems to me to mean taking on a profession in which character may well be the most important ingredient for success. All of us, but perhaps young people more even than older members of a congregation, will judge the integrity of a pastor's message by the integrity of the person behind it. Preaching the profound truth of grace and reconciliation with God will mean nothing if you are not a person of grace.

God's calling on your lives is an important one, but we cannot allow it to consume us. None of us can. All of us need to commit the old line to our hearts: our work is not our own, but God's

To him, be the glory.

For Further Reflection

Ackerman's essay tells a variety of stories, but all of them, finally, have to do with trust, which is to say full confidence in the Lord's hand in our lives and the lives of our parishioners. What experiences have you had in ministry that have aided you in building your trust that God himself is in control of all of our lives?

Humility may well be the most difficult virtue because our instincts for self-interest are so basic to our characters. How can pastors build each other up in humility without breaking each other down in the process?

Some might argue that ego is an essential characteristic of any leader, any pastor. After all, when preachers stand up before a congregation, they must believe that they are speaking for God almighty. The ability to motivate others, to inspire others, has to begin with our own inspiration.

Explain how humility needs to play a role with our undying trust in God's ways? Can we be sure of ourselves and yet not sure?

CHAPTER 9

Good Shepherding: How Straying Sheep Can be Convinced to Stop Seeking Greener Pastures for a Flock that Fits and Finally Commit to a Fold

Jennifer M. Parker

Not so very long ago populations remained stable. Today, everyone moves. Individual churches, often in competition with other fellowships down the block, find their memberships shifting in and out doors that swing open and shut almost pendulum-like. Jennifer Parker claims to be among those who sometimes find it difficult to find a loving community in a church fellowship; yet, she says, ironically she often desires exactly what she's most reluctant to give. Her own story, in this essay, helps us understand what keeps individuals apart from close and blessed fellowship today—and what can bring them together.

> When he has brought out all his own, he goes on ahead of them, and his sheep follow him because they know his voice. But they will never follow a stranger; in fact, they will run away from him because they do not recognize a stranger's voice.
>
> John 10:4-5

Going to see Pastor Tommy that afternoon was harder than going to see him for the first time three years earlier. That was a voluntary drop-in from a new member; this time, it was mandatory. The minister had asked each person in the congregation to schedule an appointment to come see him in his office for a one-on-one "vision meeting" of sorts.

As I understood it, our meeting would involve a discussion of where each member was in terms of his or her spiritual growth and leadership goals. I knew from the recent teaching on Wednesday nights and preaching on

Sundays that the pastor had been developing a theme—that of calling members to a higher level of Christian commitment. I found myself putting off my meeting with him or stopping by the church to schedule it but then finding a reason to postpone even that. I didn't relish being inventoried. That was how I characterized the process—an unwelcome inventory of my inmost soul.

For weeks, I'd been telling myself it shouldn't be this difficult to go see Pastor Tommy. He's among the warmest, most personable, and obviously caring people I've ever called my pastor. The first time I attended his church, he completely broke down my formidable defenses the moment I walked in the door. I stepped into the entryway, casting about nervously in search of the person who had invited me. No sooner had I crossed the threshold than a medium-height gentleman with iron-gray hair and a youthful, dimpled face thrust his hand into mine and shook it while saying hello and introducing himself as the pastor. THE pastor. While I stammered my own name and how I was new in town and explained who had invited me—at least that's what I think I said—he leaned closer to hear my soft, timid treble, and at the same time, without a by-your-leave, reached behind my neck and turned down the inadvertently flipped collar of my blazer.

Now, where I grew up, adult strangers almost never touched each other, except to shake hands. Blushing, I lost the sense of the rest of the conversation, not so much out of embarrassment as sheer wonder. There was something so fatherly about the gesture, so naturally was it done without thought or break in the flow of words between us. Granted, I was embarrassed about the need to have my clothing adjusted; it is a hazard to be borne often by those of us who regularly forget to look in a mirror before leaving home. Still, I was not as embarrassed as I might otherwise have been because Pastor Tommy effectively communicated with his simple, offhand gesture that in this house I was welcome as part of a family and that he was, among other things, just a dad.

That was not the understanding of THE PASTOR that I had from the church in which I grew up. In a small-town, rural church of a denomination that seemed to cherish a tradition of pomp and complex hierarchy among its officials, the pastor and presiding bishops, elders, and whatnots were people who kept their distance and took for granted the honors and privileges of the pulpit. In a small, country church congregation like the one to which my family belonged, any of those officials was regarded like royalty—visiting royalty—because they did not live among us. The higher clerical officials only gathered regionally for conferences or occasionally came to oversee the resolution of some local financial matter.

The pastor was a visitor to our community as well. He always drove to our church from his home someplace far away to preside over worship services for us on first and third Sundays. We knew he had at least one other church that got his seconds and fourths. We also knew he was temporary; he was a gift from those (to me) faceless district officials who had assigned him to our church. At a whim, they could remove him, replacing him with some novel and perhaps novice preacher. The name and face of the man in the pulpit of my childhood church changed from time to time, so it would have been difficult to get to know any of those pastors well, even if his exalted rank and aura of spiritual authority did not preclude friendship between him and a mere congregant.

However, Pastor Tommy gently insisted on knowing and being known. Equally endearing were his active, personal concern for his members (he once surprised me by showing up to visit me in the hospital when I hadn't thought anyone at church even knew I was there) and his folksy humor, which included a seemingly endless supply of really silly jokes and homespun puns that he did not consider at all unworthy of the pulpit. The charismatic (in every sense) minister delivered sermons that were very much like his conversations, full of Scripture and serious exhortation seasoned with laughter and warmth. Meanwhile, in those sermons, he often drew a peculiar distinction, lamenting in his heartfelt way, "For some of you, I'm just your preacher, not your pastor. I want to be your pastor, but you won't let me."

Pastor Tommy also encouraged responses from his congregants, even while he was preaching. In a typical extempore deviation from his notes, he would turn to this-or-that church member and ask the person to prompt him with details of a funny conversation or exciting incident he wanted to share with the rest of us. I had to learn not to be startled whenever he would call my name in recounting an anecdote or address me directly from the pulpit to affirm some detail he thought I might know. He was a pastor who made it hard to lie low; his gaze reached the whole room, penetrating even unto the back row of the sanctuary floor seating or the furthermost pew in the balcony.

I loved my pastor dearly, but I doubted that he knew it. Perhaps that is because, in spite of my love and respect for him, in the past year my attendance had slackened, my participation dropped off, and I had been considering a move to another area, which would necessarily mean a move to another church. Not knowing how to broach these subjects with him or explain my restlessness was making it hard for me to face the man I had learned to call, meaningfully, "my pastor."

Straying Sheep: Reasons for Forsaking the Assembly

It was with good reason that the apostle Paul admonished believers to "... consider how we may spur one another on toward love and good deeds. Let us not give up meeting together, as some are in the habit of doing..." (Hebrews 10:24-25). There have always been those in the household of faith who find it far easier to seek God's face in quiet, isolated contemplation and personal spiritual disciplines than in corporate worship and joint endeavor. For many such people, pride or intellectual/spiritual vanity can lead them to look outside the "simple" teachings of some churches. For others, solitude is a temptation that can manifest itself, at times, as a vice. Those so afflicted prefer to work out their own salvation beyond the context of fellowship, never realizing that this disobedience to the scriptural mandate of mutual, caring community can lead to selfishness, self-righteousness, and spiritual atrophy.

Meanwhile, other Christians may fall into the habit of avoiding the assembly out of boredom—or because they feel they are not being spiritually or emotionally fed. Hence, they rationalize that they are "getting more" out of other activities elsewhere, and if their tendency to go elsewhere remains unchecked, it increases from occasion to habit to general rule. Whether these individuals eventually fall away from their church and go looking for another, or whether they retain membership in a church they visit only on holidays and special occasions, their complacency with an unsatisfying relationship to the body where they have or had their membership is disturbing. Some might call it a sin.

Also, from Paul's day to this, there have always been those who, for various reasons, find themselves estranged from the body life of the church, whether they are marginalized by circumstances (temporary or long term), by stigma (real or imagined), or by some other sense of not fitting in. Even in the midst of a well-intentioned congregation, some members and seekers often come and go, feeling like lost sheep, wandering in a wilderness of unintentional unwelcome, unhelpful spiritual platitudes, and vague, unpenetrating goodwill. Some of the friendliest churches, many with genuinely hospitable people posted in their foyers to greet members and visitors alike with a smile and a handshake, leave the "welcomed" with nothing more lasting than the momentary glow of having been accosted by a warm Wal-Mart greeter. Yet, Scripture hints at a body life marked by intimacy to a degree almost unimaginable in this wary age, a church where those in peaceful fellowship and accord—"greet one another with a holy kiss" (2 Cor. 13:12).

In contemporary America, that level of intimacy is probably strange to most and certainly, in some aspects, not even desirable to many of us. What is desirable is a sense of being at home in the body of Christ, anchored, ready to stay and make commitments and contributions based on trust and mutuality.

I believe the churches in which spiritual and social strays find a sense of belonging and "at-homeness" are those that help their people engage with the communion of saints on the level of love and accountability that Scripture suggests is possible. It takes sensitive shepherding to bring people in from the margins of the community—or from even greater emotional distances—especially in a society where, for so many of us, past abuses and disappointments have made trust a scarce commodity. Such shepherding need not be the sole responsibility of the pastor, but it often must begin with the congregation's leader, if it is to be incorporated into the outreach philosophy of a church.

Commitment Phobia and the Call to Community

It is odd—and difficult—for me to confess that I find responding to the biblical call to community challenging, particularly when I have been such a drum-thumper for the idea of Christian community in the past. Having lived in community (i.e., communally in one household) with other Christian adults during my 20s, I've concluded that it was altogether the most spiritually healthy lifestyle I've ever led.

In the years since, as a single, working Christian adult, I've become increasingly busy, increasingly socially disengaged from local fellow believers, and increasingly solitary in my approach to worship and godliness. Meanwhile, I've been so disgruntled over what I saw as contemporary society's "severely community-challenged" state that I hardly had the presence of mind to realize that I myself was becoming more curmudgeonly and commitment-phobic with each passing year.

My adult life as a believer has been marked by place-specific ministry and characterized by movement. That is, working for church and parachurch organizations and Christian publications over the years has, along with my pursuit of academic and vocational goals, moved me through an uncommon variety of settings and circumstances. I've sojourned among many diverse church communities, both denominational and nondenominational, from the vivaciously charismatic to the spiritually sedate and from the outrageously fundamentalist to the outlandishly funky.

My environs have changed from season to whimsical season over the years in a way that reminds me of colorful, exotic scenes on a child's travel-themed View Master reel—each new scene clicking and sliding into place and then out again, with plenty of *déjà vu* as I find myself, in one way or another, coming full circle again and again. One moment I'm seeing a homey scene from a neighborhood cookout in Jackson, Mississippi (during my Antioch Community and Voice of Calvary Fellowship years); next, a picturesque Boston-area winterscape (from the intellectually stimulating and sometimes ideologically scary days when I worked at the Episcopal Divinity School/Weston Jesuit School of Theology Library). Here's a golden autumn morning in Pasadena (that I visited while doing some personal research at Fuller Theological Seminary); and now a brisk, wind-swept spring afternoon in Grand Rapids, Michigan (where I was employed with the publishing arm of the Christian Reformed Church). I have changed bases and missions repeatedly over the years, each short- or long-term camping place bringing me into a new worship community, a new sphere of ministry and influence, and yet another temporary home.

There are many benefits, but also several drawbacks to being a vagabondservant, especially as one ages and sees friends find their career and community niches, marry and have children, and generally settle into what looks, at least from one's own vantage, like a normal life. One may long for a similar earthly intimation of heaven's permanence. One does get lonely. One's arms or lap may feel empty and make one a little jealous of the easy, physical affection between parents and their children. They may take their access to hugs and goodnight kisses for granted, but the single-without-children generally do not.

Still, moments of loneliness or envy aside, I choose to pursue Christian singlehood (i.e., celibate and faith-centered, as I define it) rather than marriage. I have come to question my capacity for the sacrifices of marriage and for the long-term stability those sacrifices might provide. Sometimes I muse over whether I may have missed God or ignored his voice in my ramblings or whether I was perhaps meant to settle and put down roots a long time ago. Even as I ponder whether I'm actually called to this itinerant existence of mine, or whether I simply default to it due to an insatiably curious and restless nature, I really cannot visualize any other way of life for me.

Over time, I have learned to reserve much of the energy I once poured into new relationships and to draw concentric circles around myself, allowing people at different levels of familiarity and trust to approach me up to the point deemed wise for each—just so far and no farther. After all, relationships are, like nearly everything in this world, temporary. Why risk investing emotion and possibly being hurt? It is only lately, as I near age 40, that I have begun to look back across the years of my life and wonder exactly when I started to cluck and grow feathers.

How, when, and why did I become such a commitment-phobic, needy as I am for fellowship and the other blessings of community? Why do I move from town to town or state to state every two to five years? Why have I left so many churches that I loved and in which I believed I was growing spiritually? Also, why is it that I have kept the ministers in my life, whom I have deeply respected and even loved, at arm's length, retreating from them when they make any significant effort to minister to me in a personal way? Yes, I am single, without dependents and fairly unattached; and yes, my line of work can necessitate frequent relocation; but certainly there are other people with better reasons to keep running from place to place.

Letting the Shepherd in When the Wolf Has Been at the Door

I'm reminded of a woman I know named Jillian (not her real name), a single mother with young children, and the victim of severe emotional and physical abuse at the hands of a series of men. She moved from church to church for years, sometimes because she needed distance from another bad relationship and sometimes because she had unspecified misgivings about a pastor or ministerial staff member's interest in her. The church into which she finally was able to settle did not have the denominational label or the worship style she'd been accustomed to in the past, but she loved it there. When I asked her why, she recalled an incident that suggested her decision to join that church had boiled down to a single gesture that brought her well-fortified trust barrier down like the walls of Jericho.

"The pastor there, Reverend Morris, is a good man," she told me. "Once, I was having a real hard time making rent and buying groceries. My child support case was stalled, and my government check had gone astray because of my change of address. But since I had just moved there and started going to that church, I didn't want people all up in my business. So I didn't say anything to anybody at the church; but I guess the Holy Spirit let somebody there know I was struggling."

A soft look stole across her face as she remembered the day she got a call from the church secretary, a woman about her age, named Lois. She told Jillian the pastor had voiced concerns about "the trial she was going through." Then the secretary told her Rev. Morris had given her instructions to take Jillian shopping and get whatever food and household items she needed for herself and the kids, and to pay for it out of the church's Mercies and Outreach Ministry fund.

"I thanked her," Jillian said, "but I asked her how the minister knew I was having trouble."

She says Lois replied mysteriously, "He's a Spirit-filled man, and sometimes he just knows things, like when people are going through something."

Jillian felt as though the pastor had known more than that. She suspected that he had sensed, by the Holy Spirit or through keen observation, or some combination of the two, just how fragile her faith in people was after so many bad experiences with men.

Jillian also believed the pastor had intuited that she would have been suspicious if he or any other man in the church had approached her to express concern or ask what she needed. Desperate as she was, the welfare mom and abuse survivor might have downplayed her need and refused the help, or might even have stopped coming to the worship services, feeling uncomfortable about having attracted the minister's attention. Rev. Morris, though, had realized what he was doing, and instead of approaching her himself he had dispatched the kind and efficient Lois, who took care of the mission with tact and discretion.

The sensitive way the pastor had delegated this much needed outreach inspired Jillian, all at once, with an unfamiliar feeling of trust. Soon afterward, she began formal steps to become an official member of the congregation. Also, within a few months she started training to become a part of the church's Mercies and Outreach Ministry team, with a personal mission to start some special programs for single mothers as well as abuse victims.

When "Leave Them Alone and They'll Come Home" Doesn't Work

Thinking of Rev. Morris' soft touch reminds me of another minister of exceptional integrity and sensitivity, who has occasionally had his gentle efforts to pastor his people rebuffed. This man, Pastor Joe, even lost his flock once when his careful admonition to

a cohabiting couple in his congregation caused the two errant members to take offense and then take action to have him removed from his post.

Years later, while pastoring another church, he found himself faced with a similar situation. A couple in his congregation—Brenda and Mark—was living together, had done so for some twenty years without benefit of marriage, and even had children together.

They simply had never "gotten around to getting married," and had no such plans. After a time of prayerful soul-searching, Pastor Joe "set his face" to address the matter, counseling the man and the woman privately, separately, and together. In his caring and noncondemning way, he told them, "God's way is always the best way." He urged them to consecrate their union.

Careful probing revealed that Brenda deeply desired God's blessing on her relationship to Mark; alone with the pastor, she confessed in tears how much she wanted to be a bride. Mark also turned out to be surprisingly willing to be led in the matter.

This time, rather than being offended or leaving—or insisting that their pastor leave—the couple chose to marry, and even included their children in the ceremony, which Pastor Joe performed. He once recalled to me that he was amazed at the way God's grace shone throughout that ordeal—for he saw it as a test for him as well as for the couple. He also recalls how the look of joy on Brenda's face—and the solemn pride on Mark's—as she walked down the aisle added an extra dimension of holiness to what was already, by definition, a sacrament.

Standing on the Rock, Faithful to the Flock

Then there is my friend Alexis (again, not her real name). After growing up middle class in San Francisco and graduating from an eastern school with an Ivy League-caliber education, she relocated into a poverty-blighted urban neighborhood with a racial and socioeconomic makeup vastly different from her own. A thoughtful, articulate woman of European and Asian-American descent, Alexis had accepted Christ as a young adult and, as often happens, saw her new faith mix with her youthful energy and idealism in a somewhat combustible way.

When a couple of ministry leaders from Jackson, Mississippi, visited Alexis's university campus in Massachusetts to talk about racial justice, healing, and reconciliation, as well as the Christian mandate to serve the poor, she responded not merely with cheers and loose change but with commitment and real change—major life change. Like any biblical disciple, she left the nets of the career path she'd been prepared to follow and instead cast in with Christ.

Alexis went about seeking the Lord's will for her life by committing herself to outreach and service in an impoverished inner-city community scarred by crime, poverty, ongoing economic injustice, and a living legacy of racism endowed by years of ugly history. She joined a racially mixed but majority African-American congregation and found herself frustrated at times by the mistrust that existed, even in the body of Christ, among people divided by the artificial boundary lines of race and class and gender.

Alexis had to get used to apologizing, especially when her intentions were simply misunderstood. She had to learn to temper her progressive idealism with knowledge and experience—to let this Southern urban community's recognized issues and felt needs come before her own priorities on the justice agenda. She even bit her tongue most of the time while listening to community members assert that feminism is not an evangelical issue or that the recognition of women's gifts in Christian ministry is not as important to black women as the need to have their men take a stronger leadership role in the church.

Meanwhile, the ex-Californian poured herself into the life of her Mississippi church's target neighborhood. She worked at various times on the staff or the board of four different church-affiliated ministries in the community. She volunteered at a local soup kitchen and other community outreaches. She conducted an after-school Bible club for kids on her street and hosted an adult small-group Bible study, both in her home. At her church, she sang in the choir, played on the women's softball team, and even accepted, under protest, a leading role in the Easter musical one year.

Sometimes Alexis felt used, abused, burned out, and ready to quit her church and nearly everything associated with it, except maybe some of the people. Often she bristled over the "old fashioned," sexist, and set-in-their-ways thinking and preaching of the pastor and other men on the church's ministerial staff. Many times she felt woefully alone, even in the midst of all her involvement and activity, especially as she saw so many other young adult members leave the church, either to move far away or to find a local church home elsewhere, perhaps in a less challenging setting.

I was one of those who left. Though I stayed in touch, I marveled at the fact that my Anglo-Chinese American, San Franciscan-born, adult-convert Christian friend had become more thoroughly integrated into—and read that as "integral to" and "showing more integrity toward"—that African-American, Mississippi church and community than I, a native black Mississippian raised in a Christian home, ever did or ever could have.

Alexis did leave her church for a season, staying on in the area but remaining unaffiliated and visiting other congregations. However, she eventually returned.

Asked why, she talked about how she found that, no matter what the congregation's problems were, she could not turn her back on the people with whom she had already shared so much of her life. Also, she found that over time she had developed a relationship with her pastor that allowed for increasing candor. The more she was able to tell him what she thought about various church matters—about the leadership and administrative structure of the church, its fellowship and relationship issues, race and gender inequities, and even her problems with his sermons—the more he solicited her feedback.

Alexis was gratified to see many things gradually change in the church, in part as a result of her input. She saw a slow, steady growth of mutual trust between the pastor and other congregants and herself; and she saw her own increased influence as a leader in her church, a harvest of carefully, faithfully sown seeds of commitment and trust.

My friend, who is a never-married single like me, has lived in her urban Mississippi community and has belonged to her church there (excepting that brief interval of disassociation) for more than a quarter of her life now. She has contributed there and made a difference in ways she would never bother to enumerate; nor would it be easy for anyone else to count them.

I submit her experience in contrast to my own. If I ever become impatient with the amount of trust, responsibility, or leadership opportunity extended to me in my own church, I have only to consider the amount of trust I have placed in my fellow church members and leaders, the level of commitment I have made to them, or even the amount of time I have spent with them and invested in them, in comparison to the details of Alexis's story.

Of course, I have never aspired to be the mover-and-shaker that Alexis is by nature. Slow to commit to anything that will require any long-term involvement, I tend to volunteer for tasks that require a low level of responsibility, not much time, and not much risk.

Some of my wariness about church commitment I chalk up to my early years of membership in a church in which the relationship between members and leaders was not one of trust and was in fact barely a relationship at all. It's ironic that I've become every bit as untrustworthy a church member as those pastors who came and went over the years.

Then, too, lack of confidence has been an issue. Added to my poor follow-through record is a poor self-assurance, with little confidence in my voice and less in my ability to assert anything important or to exercise any spiritual authority. Thanks to these handicaps, it has been hard for me to see myself in church leadership roles, let alone actually to perform well in them when I happen to accept one.

In the past, I've attributed much of my sense of inadequacy and self-distrust to my socialization as a woman in a predominately male-affirming if not male-dominated culture and church, where the norms were male assertiveness and female submissiveness. After all, I grew up in the very nonfeminist social context that my friend Alexis has only invaded relatively lately with all her liberal ideals and Christian feminist enlightenment. However, Pastor Tommy surprised me early in our acquaintance by going against what I thought of as the cultural grain of our milieu.

When I talked with the minister about the hesitancy and self-doubt the Apostle Paul's mandate to "let your women be silent in church" inspired in me, Pastor Tommy told me that, as a single woman, "you are the priest of your home." He went on to encourage me to recognize that I am called to Christian leadership as much as any believer, whether or not that call included ordained ministry—another matter on which he was willing to prove himself biblically counter-cultural, if need be. Then the pastor went on to assure me that I would not be usurping authority over anyone if I exercised my "priesthood of all believers" rights to speak scripturally and prophetically, as long as this was done "in order" at the proper time and place and with the right heart.

Those words continued to work in my spirit long after Pastor Tommy uttered them. His exhortation engendered a sense of responsibility that would not leave me alone—responsibility to do and be more, to know and to teach more, and to grow more into my role as a leader in the church and a lay minister of the gospel of Jesus Christ.

Where to begin, though—that was the hard part, and not because I didn't have any idea. As a one-time member of the Christian household fellowship known as Antioch in Jackson, Mississippi, I had learned what genuine community required of a person: commitment, confession, submission, accountability, forgiveness, grace, and love—more love than is humanly possible. That is why the apostle Paul wrote:

> For this reason I kneel before the Father, from whom his whole family in heaven and on earth derives its name. I pray that out of his glorious riches he may strengthen you with power through his Spirit in your inner being, so that Christ may dwell in your hearts through faith. And I pray that you, being rooted and established in love, may have power, together with all the saints, to grasp how wide and long and high and deep is the love of Christ, and to know this love that surpasses knowledge—that you may be filled to the measure of all the fullness of God. (Eph. 3:14-19)

Finally, I mustered the courage to set and keep the appointment. I went to Pastor Tommy's office at the church with a slight sinking feeling because I knew that my straying sheep's heart was already dreaming of going off wandering across the hills, but something told me that before I finished talking with the man of God he would have convinced me that this church is where I belong, that the Lord brought me there for a reason. I knew he would lay out his vision for the congregation in such a way that I would see, through his eyes, my place in it. I also knew that, before I left his office, I would have committed to one or more tasks, or a series of tasks of increasing difficulty. I went, knowing something would be required of me, something more than I'd given up to now, and because I love the pastor, I knew that I would give it.

It all happened pretty much as I expected. Pastor Tommy welcomed me with a handshake and averred that it had made his day when he heard I was coming. Sitting down on the overstuffed sofa in his study, I leaped into a confession, apologizing for having let my career distractions and extended family issues (my care for elderly parents and a divorced sibling with four kids at home) keep me from more regular attendance. I confessed, too, that I felt many of my gifts had no place in our church.

I acknowledged that I'd let frustration over this apparent fact fester into hurt pride, which led me to take my gifts to venues outside the church. "I'm over-committed beyond these walls," I explained, "and I think I let myself get that way because I felt bitter that I've had trouble finding a way to use the best of my gifts here. No one seemed to need what I had to offer, so I've taken it elsewhere."

Pastor Tommy was sympathetic but encouraging. He accepted my confession and apology, expressing genuine concern over a few recent small troubles of mine—family illnesses, housing and financial challenges, work and transportation issues. But as for my complaint about finding no place for my gifts in the church, he negated the notion with vehemence and talked excitedly about a writing project of his, on which he hoped to solicit my help. He also talked about the new, larger sanctuary for which the congregation is raising funds, and all the ways it would enable our church to expand its teaching ministry and outreach—and how that would provide opportunities for me and others to share what God is showing us.

"I like to preach and teach and minister to my people from the Word," Pastor Tommy said, "but I also like to let y'all minister back to me. Sometimes what God is showing one of you can be a revelation to me that just blows my mind. So if He is speaking something into your life, I want you to share that with me from time to time. Maybe you could e-mail me some of your articles and things."

I smiled, half at his colorful way of speaking and half at the heart that his words revealed. He asked me if anything else was on my mind, and I timidly suggested that I felt called to explore in greater depth the private and social significance of Communion. I asked him, doctrinally speaking, what he thought about the idea of a lay person reverently serving communion to an intimate gathering of church friends in a small group setting at home. He applauded the idea, and gave me his blessing to do as I was led in that matter.

I was breathing easier, feeling the viselike grip of commitment phobia loosening. Instead of requiring a lot of things of me, the pastor had given me permission to follow the Holy Spirit and expand my horizons, not by running away, but by running ahead, further up the path toward where this Christian fellowship of believers was headed.

My relationship to him makes it easier to see myself doing that. There are many things that I won't do for a cause or an ideal, but that I will do for a person. When my pastor speaks to me, I am honored by his confidence in what I can add to the body of Christ, and that is ultimately a big part of what keeps me hanging around. I like to think I am a solid enough believer that I could serve Christ just about anywhere; but when he gives me people that I can love and respect and even, wayward as I am, follow it is a strong indicator that those people are the ones the Lord is calling me to be around, at least for the present.

The Word says that to be absent from the body is to be present with the Lord. To be present with the body—the body of Christ, that is—is to be present with the Lord's people, investing yourself in their future and enjoying a give and take among a community of faith that is like the flawed prototype of a perfect schematic. Stray or stay, I am reminded by my time with my pastor that no promise is being exacted of me that is anything more than my part of a mutual covenant of caring and relationship.

I love my pastor. I love my fellow congregants, especially when I see them through his eyes. When I hear him talk about the present and future needs of the church and my part in fulfilling them, I can even almost love the scary sound of the fold gate shutting tight. At this moment, by the grace of God, I am choosing to stay with the flock ... for now.

For Further Reflection

These days, especially in the evangelical world, people sometimes refer to the "circulation of the saints" as opposed to the "communion of the saints." What does Parker's essay help us understand about the motivations of those who move from one fellowship to another?

How can the church minister to men and women who, like Parker, are often so busy with their lives outside of church that they neither look for nor find much community within? Comment on this idea: "Sometimes the best ministry for some people is simply to leave them alone."

Parker calls herself a "commitment-phobic." Is there a paradox here? Is it fair to say that some people who really desire close community are, at the same time, unwilling to give themselves to such a community? How prevalent is that attitude today?

Is it possible for pastors not to see members leaving their fellowships as a personal affront?

How can pastors effectively gauge and respond to the level of genuine relationship (i.e., intimacy, involvement, and accountability) members are seeking or are ready for? How do you communicate concern for individuals in your church? Does your relational style communicate an invitation to greater intimacy with church members?

CHAPTER 10

The Greatest of These

James Calvin Schaap

The central command of all of scriptural revelation is the directive we are given to love—God almighty first, then our neighbors as ourselves. After a humorous fable about a well-meaning church looking for just the right new under shepherd, James Calvin Schaap uses stories from his own church experience to shed light on just how pastors might follow that central command, which is, of course, "the greatest of these."

Calling: A Story

When Pastor Rog left Springvale Church, there was no weeping or gnashing of teeth. Not that he and the members of his congregation didn't get along. Pastor Rog was easy to like—after all, everyone agreed on that. In addition, he followed the rules, even those left totally unstated. He wore the right clothes and sent his kids to the right schools. He held memberships in the Lions club *and* the C of C, which meant he kept an active and public life as a volunteer, and, thereby, did a great job keeping up a presence for Springvale in the city. His wife had a respectable part-time job at a local nursing home. His kids were well behaved.

That the people of Springvale Church weren't sorry to see Pastor Rog leave had nothing to do with his sociability, his family, his personality, or his willingness to work. It had to do with his preaching—which was, most reviews stated, at best, ho-hum. Pastor Rog's pursuit of texts was, well, plodding, as was his general delivery. He rarely deviated from six or eight favorite gestures (a tightly clenched fist turned inward was his favorite), and he tended to repeat the phrase, *in large part*, so frequently that kids regularly tallied the numbers and compared notes afterward. His sermons, many of the good Springvale souls claimed, seemed predictable—which was to say, boring.

However, the Springvale congregation would not have been so eager to see him leave if they had been aware of the complex process of locating a suitable replacement. The church hadn't been without a preacher since before the war—at least that's what people claimed, although no one knew exactly which war people meant when they said that. Finding a new under shepherd, the council noted in its July meeting, would be a challenge demanding the best from everyone.

At that same meeting, they decided that before selecting candidates for the new job, they would survey needs and wants by making a survey of the church's various groups and societies.

By the following Tuesday, Brother Morse (a computer programmer by trade) prepared a fourteen-page questionnaire, which the council subsequently distributed, calling it an "assessment instrument." They gave members a strict deadline for completing and returning the survey. In August, most of the congregation's various interest groups spent quality time discussing the type of pastor the Springvale congregation needed. The council wanted results by September.

Meanwhile, the council devoted its entire August meeting to drawing a profile, beginning with this note—"we don't believe Springvale is ready for a woman pastor." Thusly, the pronouns were masculine. He has to be charismatic, they said, and scriptural, capable of writing and speaking not only fluently but with requisite passion; he should have a strong pastoral heart, be a compassionate listener; and he must be committed to kingdom work, gifted with intelligence; a man who is wise with a gracious heart. A good place to begin, they thought.

That profile, the consistory concluded, brought only one candidate to mind. If they were to call someone without the congregation's approval—in fact, were they that very night to call the man of their choice—it would be, by unanimous vote, King David, an extraordinary leader, practiced in the arts, and the man God himself described as "closest to my heart."

It was determined, however, that their assessment should be kept confidential so as not to weigh upon various other groups' decision-making.

Sadly, someone leaked the results to the Phoebe Society, who, as requested, spent their August meeting drawing up their own agenda. "King David certainly has much to commend him," they maintained in a twenty-page document filed less than two weeks after the instrument had been distributed. However, because of "the Bathsheba incident," his "credulity with women" suffered tremendously. "Therefore," said the members of the Phoebe Society, "we're opposed to nominating David as our new pastor." Such a nomination, they insisted, revealed a rather "obvious disregard" for women's issues.

Instead, the Phoebe Society recommended that, if a woman pastor wasn't going to be possible at this point in time, the congregation should call Jacob's son, Joseph, a man who clearly had not stumbled as David had—

even when proffered the possibility. Furthermore, he had shown great compassion in distributing foodstuffs to the needy during his tenure as Egypt's Secretary of Agriculture. What's more, he'd willingly bared his emotions—his tears fell easily—when finally opening himself up to his supplicant brothers. "We believe that Joseph is the best candidate to replace Pastor Rog," they offered in their own summary conclusions.

The Men's Society, the organization with the highest median age in the congregation, brawled over which of the Old Testament prophets showed greatest promise. After six ballots, they nominated Jeremiah, even though there was much discussion about whether or not the man too frequently repeated himself. The Society's second choice was Isaiah who, they claimed, despite some really beautiful verse, lacked the requisite tenacity. They liked Hosea, but claimed there were some lingering questions about his ability to keep his house in order. Theirs was, by the way, the only instrument completed in longhand.

The youth pastor's response came on his own personal stationery, festooned with unicorns. He claimed that calling any one of the woe-speaking prophets would be the kind of move that would be sure to alienate teens. The candidate most likely to find a place in the hearts of his kids, he maintained, would be the father of the prodigal son—although he wasn't sure anymore whether a rancher could make it with city kids. If it had to be someone prophetlike, the youth pastor said, Balaam and his talking ass were the kind of act that would keep everyone's attention. "What a hoot that would be," he wrote, adding three exclamation points. "You'd never know what he was going to say. They'd love it." Then a smiley face.

The Circle, a support group composed mainly of single individuals, made a rather convincing case for calling the Samaritan woman. However, because a woman pastor was not a possibility, they recommended the apostle Paul, who, despite his sometimes-virulent sexism, seemingly understood very well the dignity of the single life.

Support for Jonah came from post-high schoolers who rarely came to church, except when dragged along by their parents. Although quite unorganized (they submitted no formal document), they were unofficially polled by one of the elders while standing out on the sidewalk after the morning service. "Jonah?" Elder Dominick said, nonplussed, "—because of the whale business?"

"Yah, that too," one of them said. "But mostly, that vine thing—I love that. You know—'been there, done that.'"

The apostle Paul was the second choice of the men of the Breakfast Club, the business leaders who met biweekly at the health club, where, in addition to playing racquetball doubles, they ate thickly granola-ed yogurt and studied the greatest hits of C. S. Lewis. The apostle Paul had some appeal—"running the race and all of that," but John the disciple got the nod because, not only was he was the finest athlete of the twelve, he found a gracious way to make his athleticism clear in the story of the resurrection.

The club's other vote went to Daniel, who, they claimed, was the most intelligent of all the prophets; well-educated in the ways of the world; obviously committed to the faith; and, good night, what endurance, they said.

The small groups got together to discuss their needs but claimed they didn't feel up to naming a specific candidate. They'd be likely to approve of anyone, they said, as long as he or she was there at Pentecost.

The Reach-out Committee threw in a strong vote for Elijah, assuming he could pull off a stunt like the one on Mt. Carmel, for those eight hundred prophets of Baal.

The *Christianity Today* Discussion Group thought maybe they could get John the Baptist; but they said they'd work on the clothing thing if it all worked out. The *Christian Century* group were sure the only fit candidate was the Ethiopian because Springvale was so disturbingly monochrome. Like the Men's Society, the Dobson-ites wanted Jeremiah, but claimed they could settle for any of his immediate Old Testament neighbors.

Al-Anon wasn't given to naming names but claimed they could live with Noah—or, for that matter, any of his sons.

The Liturgy Committee felt Moses would be a good man to decide once and for all the laws governing good music and proper worship styles, but they claimed they'd consider Solomon, too, if he'd promise to shed some of the darkness of Ecclesiastes. Then, someone brought up the concubines, and they determined he wouldn't be a good choice, not in the present ecclesiastical climate. Finally, they settled on Noah, too, even though they claimed to know very little about his worship preferences. "Anyone who could keep order on the ark has great potential," they said.

The senior choir liked King David a lot, too, but felt anything less than J. S. Bach would be a disappointment. The junior choir, who didn't read the instructions, voted en masse for Casting Crowns.

The Sunday school wanted Noah, too, as long as the animals were part of the deal.

The janitor, incredibly, voted for Mr. Clean—if you can believe it.

At its October meeting, the consistory read through all the documents and recommendations. They wrote the names of the candidates on the chalkboard, listing some of the attributes each would bring to the job. Then they started calling. They called and called and called again, but for the most part—aside from a brief, unenthusiastic conversation with a strange man named J. S. Bach in Belvedere, they got absolutely nowhere—couldn't even talk to a machine.

Finally, one of the elders, Mr. Brummel, wiped his forehead in the late summer heat and recommended giving a man named William Sands a call.

No one moved.

Brummel explained that when he was on vacation in a little resort town up state he had heard the man preach. Better than passable, Brummel said.

The idea seemed preposterous.

"Nice family. Good smile. Warm." Brummel hunched his shoulders.

The entire room sat in grave silence.

"Well, I don't know," Brummel said. "I guess I just found him really nice—you know, a good heart—human?"

"Human?" they said in chorus.

"Told a joke once or twice—the people liked him," he said. "Yeah, human."

There were misgivings, but that night, fearful of paralysis, the consistory extended the call. Some members chose to reserve their approval, but a few months later Pastor Sands arrived in Springvale—encouragingly nervous but eager.

Alas, all is not well in Springvale. Some people don't believe William Sands has the qualities they wanted in a minister. In fact, after hearing three sermons, the support group for reformed, ex-lottery players has already made book on his tenure. They're giving him two years, at 3 to 1 odds.

****

Some people say the novel is dead because in today's complex world only nonfiction is rangy enough to grasp what we have to know. They may be right. Perhaps the little story you just read is much ado about very little—I simply could have written, I suppose, that congregations want pastors of biblical proportions, when it's simply impossible. I mean, Elijah pulls off one of the most memorable grandstand events in the history of revelation and almost immediately falls into depression. Talk about bi-polar. The man would have never passed seminary screening.

In my church life—which includes more than a half century, three terms as an elder, and two horrific congregational battles—what experiences can I marshal to begin to answer a difficult question: What makes a good pastor?

No more fiction, but I'll try to answer in the best way I know how, by way of stories.

Respect, Which is Love

Well, duh. Hardly a Solomon-worthy subtitle. Let me try to explain.

A friend of mine who has worked in corporations his entire life claims that he can sit in the office of a business for ten minutes and get a feel for the spirit of the culture within. I've been in dozens and dozens of high school rooms throughout my life as a guest. I need to be in the door for only a few minutes to know whether the next fifty will be, for me, a joy or a death sentence.

Recently, I was asked to read stories in a tiny rural church, where I met a pastor who seemed younger than my own son. He was single, not broad-shouldered or about to be featured in *GQ*. I sat at a dinner table with him and some of the older members of his congregation, ate the requisite ham steak and mashed potatoes, and knew almost immediately that there existed between them a nearly divine relationship. You can see it in the eyes.

Why? Let me call it "measured passion." When I asked this young pastor about the congregation, he was excited, even though in seminary he'd likely never dreamed he'd spend his first years so far out in the hinterland. Good things were happening in this dying town of less than five hundred souls, he told me, big things; those grandmas at our table basked in his joy. He loved his job. His passion was obvious.

He also loved *them*—let me rephrase that: He *respected* them. He listened when they spoke, he gave them his eyes and his full attention, even though much of the conversation was the kind of small talk we, like the travelers to Emmaus, employ with out-of-town guests at our meals. He listened to them, and they knew that they were affirmed.

Will he have problems someday? I've got no crystal ball. Even King David had his bad days—and nights. However, the atmosphere in that fellowship hall was alive with respect, and for me, the guest, it was a joy to be there.

A requirement of good pastoring is the respect necessary to listen, and that respect is attributable, I think, to love. In my experience, good pastors love their parishioners and show it by respect.

Trust, Which is Love

In my first term as elder—lo, many years ago—I was sent, along with one of my colleagues, to visit with a young couple whose timing was off. She was pregnant, and they weren't married. Every writer who has come from the Christian Reformed Church has dealt with the denomination's sordid history of public confessions of the sin against the seventh commandment; I'm not interested in revisiting our sad past by telling this story. You may think such a visit we took to be barbaric—that's okay, but we were sent to visit this young unmarried couple, just to visit.

What occasionally happened back then was that the professor on the team—that's me—ended up, by default, the official voice, even though I was the new kid around the consistory table. My associate during this visit was, and still is, a fine man, a good man, but a day laborer who, like many others, simply assumed that professors were gifted with words.

That night, however, my colleague did all the talking, which surprised me. When he told them what he did, I realized that the conversation belonged in other hands than mine; it really belonged to God.

The two young people were sitting cozily on a couch, a worn-out monster that sat so low we were looking at their knees. Neither of them was talkative, more than a bit intimidated by institutional righteousness of an official church visit.

"I want you to know," my partner said after a few formalities, "that it happened to me too—me and my wife, so I know how you feel right now." He nodded graciously.

That was news, and the professor was struck dumb.

"It happened to my own kids, too," he went on. "I want you to know that it hurt me a lot more when it happened to my kids than when it happened to me," he said, softly, gently. He looked that young couple right in the eye. "So what I want to know is this: How are you getting along with your parents?"

Those few minutes we spent with that young couple I mark as one of the most engaging visits I ever made as an elder, and for the most part I was speechless. Maybe that's why. Our pastor was nowhere to be seen, but that's where I'm going with this story. In the months and weeks prior to that couple's marriage, our pastor saw that couple frequently, I'm sure; but that night, he trusted his people to do the job.

Is such trust always successful? Wouldn't we all wish as much? He believed our visit would bring comfort and joy, and it did.

That trust, like respect, grows from and into love.

I can't help but tell another.

Only once in my life have I walked through the valley of the shadow, and that was almost two years ago, when I sat for several days at the bedside of my father who was, at that time, dying.

My father and I never really shared any final words. We never spoke in that blissful way most of us fantasize might occur in the final moments we have with those we love. I helped him when he needed to drink, when he needed to urinate, when he felt deep pain; but most often he didn't know I was there—even who was there. The intensity of the pain and the effort his body was mounting simply to stay alive drew all of his strength and will and consciousness.

One afternoon, a man came in from my father's church. He was my father's district elder, and it was his job, I know, to visit. When he came in, I told him my father likely wouldn't know he'd come. That didn't deter him. This burly guy I remember as a truck driver walked to the bedside, took my father's hand, and spoke to him as if Dad was hanging on every last word, even tried to engage him in a conversation he didn't have a chance of starting.

A big burly angel of mercy, his hair square-cut as a GI, a guy I had some trouble thinking of as an elder, a man I don't know that I'd ever spoken to before—that man looked into my father's agonized face, held my father's hand, and told him in no uncertain terms that as far as he was concerned, my father had modeled Jesus Christ in Oostburg, Wisconsin.

Then he backed away, looked at me, shook my hand, and left, wiping tears from his eyes, as was I.

I don't know whether any of that got into my father's mind. Later, the nurses told me they'd often been surprised by what people in my father's condition did hear, but I heard it—every single word of that truck driver's testimony.

"Though I walk through the valley of the shadow of death," the twenty-third says, "I will fear no evil for thou art with me." That day, God sent a truck driver.

So did the pastor.

Wisdom, Which is Love

I stumbled on a confounding problem, years ago, when two members of a congregation where I was serving as elder simply couldn't get along. What I didn't know was that what I was dealing with in their mutual anger had relatively little to do with the latest provocation.

The rule of thumb in that church, as in many older and more rural churches, was that members of a congregation who couldn't dwell in brotherhood had to straighten out their differences before there could be true Christian fellowship, which meant that they couldn't come to the Lord's Table, the bread and the wine. Those men were using that rule idea as a weapon. "With him in church, I can't take communion," they told the pastor.

Once I discovered there were decades of bad blood there, I wanted to cleanse all the detritus from the ancient conflicts, do some South African truth and reconciliation by cleaning up all history. I was young, idealistic—I was seeing dreams and wanting to make the church a blessed community.

I called an old pastor of mine, a man who'd spent the many years of his ministry in the small-town churches like ours, and asked him what I could do about purging sins from the historical record.

"In the kind of congregation you're in," he said, giggling a bit, "if you do that, all you'll be doing for the rest of your years is looking backward. Deal with today or you'll be forever dredging up history."

That wisdom was what I needed, even though I thought I had it in spades.

"Wisdom," Proverbs says, """is supreme; therefore get wisdom. Though it cost all you have, get understanding."

A member of our congregation decided a woman on the other side of the fence looked sweeter than the one he looked at nightly. The situation wasn't pretty—but then neither was he. It seemed incredible to me that a guy like that—hardly a stunner—could simply pick up another woman. I was shocked. "How on earth did that happen?" I asked my old pastor.

"They find each other," he said. "They do—if they're lookin', they find each other."

That made sense, but I was still surprised.

"I've been in this for a long time," he told me, "so long that nothing surprises me any more." He said that with a smile.

That's wisdom.

Reverence, Which is Love

It probably wasn't the first time he served communion, but our new pastor was in the middle of the sacrament one Sunday morning, when he did something stunning. In the church I attend, we have wonderful bakers who provide the congregation with beautiful loaves of bread for every celebration; our pastor, admiring the loaf itself, but far more awed by the magic we were about to experience, took a loaf from the plate, walked around the table with it in his hands, and showed it off as if it were something remarkable, which of course, it was and is. What was written on his face at that moment was sheer awe—not for the bread but for God's gift. It's remarkable how callous we can all become to the sheer miracle of the Incarnation itself, the profound mystery that the Word became flesh. Those few moments in the front of the church made clear our pastor's reverence for what he was up to, for what we can never take for granted.

I've often told my writing students that the gift of the Spirit that is prerequisite to writing is awe, the capacity to be stunned by cabbage moths, by dawn itself, by the innocence of a child, by the architecture of a snow drift. Preachers are, of course, writers.

A couple years ago, in an ancient South Dakota church, I asked a tour group to see if we could sing, without accompaniment, an old Psalter tune,

"To the Hills I Lift Mine Eyes." We'd just come through some of the most beautiful land one can imagine, following the Missouri River valley along the path Lewis and Clark took two hundred years before. It's not hard to be awed by the presence of nothingness. If you can stand somewhere and look for miles into the horizon, it's impossible not to be humbled.

There were fifty of us, maybe more, most of them a bit older than I was; and I honestly don't know where I got the idea. We stood in that old church and sang that old psalm, a patchwork of words that turned into a clear rendition only because some of us knew some of the words some of the time. We were a community.

I learned the psalms as a boy sitting in catechism at a time when it was assumed that memorization wasn't thought to be cruel and unusual punishment. In addition to having to memorize the questions and answers to the Heidelberger, our pastor mimeographed the old psalms onto legal-sized paper, and assigned them for us to memorize, week-by-week. He'd go around the class and ask us to recite.

If the truth be known, the jackets we all wore to class helped me a bit. I'd stick that long sheet of paper between the back of the chair of the kid in front of me for easy reference and likely seemed a far better student than I was.

Today, forty-plus years later, I'm happy I can sing "Zion Founded on the Mountain" and a ton of others that have all but passed from our collective memories.

I wasn't thrilled with the preacher's insistence on our memorizing when I was a kid, but he stayed at it, not because our parents demanded we have more work in catechism than we already did—memorization and tests and even catechism report cards. He stayed at it because of love for those psalms, because of passion for their importance to a Christian mind, because of awe of their beauty and importance to sanctification. I'm happy he did.

Then, there's this. The paradigm by which I've always seen the Christian life is a series of road signs that rise from the Heidelberg Catechism, the handbook of doctrine we learned—sometimes painfully—as kids. They go like this: "sin, salvation, service."

The storyline begins with sin—our knowledge of it, as it exists within us. Calvin starts even a bit earlier, with the heavens, with our sense of God as manifest in his world—what we see and experience. Because humans can't help but note God's marvelous heavens and the earth, we come to know there is, in fact, a God. With that knowledge, our own limitations surface—we certainly aren't him. There begins the knowledge of human limits—our knowledge of sin.

If we believe we are ourselves capable of fulfilling our needs, we have no need of a Savior. Thus, our conviction of sin, of our limitations, is a prerequisite to our knowing God's saving work. Sin precedes salvation, or so the story goes, through the second chapter.

Once we experience his presence, his love, we know that, in spite of our sin, he loves us anyway. Our hearts fill, our souls rejoice; we can't help but celebrate. That celebration leads us into gratitude and service, into doing what we can to be his agents of love in the world he loves so greatly.

Sin, salvation, service—that's the storyline of the narrative in which I was reared.

Mother Theresa's take on a very similar tale is a three-step process not totally unlike Heidelberg's narrative line, colored alternatively by her life in Calcutta's ghettoes. Our redemption begins in repulsion, she used to claim—what we see offends us, prompts us to look away. However, we really can't or shouldn't or won't; we have to look misery in its starving face, and when we do, we move from repulsion to compassion—away from rejection and toward loving acceptance.

There's a final chapter to Mother Theresa's narrative, what she called "bewonderment." Our compassion leads us to bewonderment.

"Bewonderment" is one of those strange words no one uses but everyone understands. It's a word like *reverence*, hard to come by in a culture where our supposed needs are never more than a price tag away.

I'll admit that bewonderment is hard to come by for me, perhaps because it isn't so clearly one of the chapters in the story I was told as a boy, a story still deeply embedded in my soul. "Service" is the end of the Christian life for me, not "bewonderment."

Maybe that's why I'm envious of David's praise in Psalms like 57, for instance, where, in his tribulation—the unjustly enraged Saul just outside the cave—he says: Be exalted, O God, above the heavens; let your glory be over all the earth" (verse 11).

What David sings to God in prayer is something I rarely tell him. I don't think I've ever asked God not to hide his light under a bushel, to display his radiant grace from pole-to-pole. Instead, I'm forever asking favors, and only rarely adoring, in part because I'm so rarely in awe.

Bewonderment is something I'm learning, and for that I'm thankful—for the book of Psalms, for David, and for the God David knew so intimately that he could speak the way he does in Psalm 57.

It's difficult for some of us to be intimate with God—to be so close to a being so great and grand and seemingly out of reach. I think it's something a song can teach—and the heavens too. It's something even an old man or woman can learn, if we have ears.

Awe, bewonderment, reverence—call it what you will, or call it love.

Perseverance, Which is Love

One long night I'll never forget happened at Rehoboth, New Mexico, when my wife and I were youth leaders at a church in Arizona. We were there for a rally. Two of us were assigned the night watch, myself and another man, a youth leader from another church. We needed to patrol because covenant children were what they were, as are we all. It was late, and things seemed settled down—two at night, or morning.

A conversation began, I remember, mostly a story my fellow hall counselor told about his father, an early missionary to the Navajo. It wasn't all that easy for him to be there, at Rehoboth again, he said. He'd been back since the days when he'd gone to school there, but not often; and just being there reminded him of what his parents put him through when he was a boy.

His father's "parish" was the reservation; every Monday morning he'd drive his children to Rehoboth, where this man, then a boy, and his sister attended school. He remembered vividly what it felt like to live in a basement room when he was six, a resident of the place. He remembered what it felt like to watch his parents return to the field, to the harvest, to the sinners needing redemption. He remembered, he said, abandonment. Anger used to flare up in him at the fact that, in some ways, he'd been denied a childhood for his father's commitment to Christian service, he told me.

I listened. "But you're here," I said. You're a youth leader, and you're here, and you've forgotten all that?"

"Took me thirty-five years," he said, a good chunk of his adult life.

"What happened?" I asked.

In those early years of his father's ministry, he said, that little reservation assembly may not have seen a single new face in five or six years, despite the fact that his father would go out to the hogans of the reservation, sleep beside campfires, trying to build relationships strong enough to break through the racial and cultural differences. His father had invested in mind, body, and soul—as had his mother. They had given everything to the preaching of the Word, even their own children.

"And you've forgiven him," I said.

"I have," he told me, "but my sister hasn't spoken to them for years."

"How did you make peace?" I said.

Many of the old Navajo his father had visited and helped, he said, the ones his father had tried to minister to had been calling in the last several years, calling the preacher when they needed him. The ancient ones were dying, some of the people in whom his father had invested so much, and they wanted his father to do funerals, to bring comfort, the solace of the Spirit.

The missionary's son made peace himself, he told me, only because it took him so long to understand why his life, his childhood, had been as misshapen as he thought it was. Only when he realized the calling his father had undertaken—even though it may have been done at his own expense—only then could he make peace.

There we were, in the darkness, outside the dorms at Rehoboth.

There's a balance here that every preacher—and all of us really—have to negotiate. The old missionary's success, like all of ours perhaps, comes with a price; and there are morals galore to be gathered from the frayed ends of the tale I was told out there on the reservation.

Believers, those committed to service in gratitude, all work mightily at maintaining balance between our various callings—as fathers and mothers, as pastors and laypeople, as people who are called to love God's world as greatly as he did, so greatly he gave his Son. The story has a warning.

It also has promise. Think of the old missionary out there beneath the stars, a colorful blanket thrown over him, a fire crackling. Think of the weeks and months and even years that passed through weekly Sabbath worship where no new face ever appeared. Imagine the perseverance simply being out there required.

Sixty years later, on or off the reservation, I'm not sure any church demands less. Hence, the little opening fable featuring our gargantuan and sometimes seemingly divine expectations.

May God help us—those of us behind the pulpit and those in the pew—to be his witnesses, in every way, in his world. All it requires of us—all of us—is love, which is, of course, the greatest of these

For Further Reflection

Schaap's opening fable portrays the kind of intimidation many pastors feel—the aspiration of a church for a pastor who is a saint—or a savior. How can pastors successfully offer their humanness to the congregations? That is, how can pastors offer the vulnerability of their humanness without undercutting the expectations coming from the pew?

Do you agree with Schaap about "bewonderment"? Does the strength and power of Reformed theology—with its emphasis on service—sometimes keep us from feeling the awe or inspiration other fellowships feel? How does a pastor nurture pew sitters in "bewonderment"?

Do you think pastors sometimes fail to trust their own leadership? If so, is that distrust born from those pastors' own desire to do things themselves, or from a fear their lay leaders won't accomplish the required tasks in the best way?

The essay's clear thesis is the absolute importance of love. How can pastors actively work at loving the people they deal with day after day?